Computer Jargon

The Illustrated Glossary of Basic Computer Terminology

Kevin Wilson

Elluminet Press
www.elluminetpress.com

Computer Jargon

Images used courtesy of the following sources and photographers: iStock.com/golibo, PeopleImages, ymgerman. Photo 130859010 © Kaspars Grinvalds - Dreamstime.com. Photo 103557713 © Konstantin Kolosov - Dreamstime.com. Yuri Arcurs via Getty Images, Chris Bardgett / Alamy Stock Photo, sto-noname/Depositphotos.com, mkos83 / arka38 / ShutterStock, SPBer, jamesgroup, Afrank99, FDominec, Fox89, FreeImages/LukeAnderson, Miguel Á. Padriñán. CC BY-SA 3.0 : Raimond Spekking 79057592, pd4u, Julianprescott2604juuly, Frettled, Dmitry Makeev, Thomas Nguyen, Konstantin Lanzet, MaXim, AlexJ, Xeper, Asier03, Santeri Viinamäki, Evan-Amos, Stefan506, grmwnr, Wolfgang Beyer, Berklas, MBlairMartin, Cliffydcw, Glavkosmoswiki, yasser ammar almasri

About the Author

With over 20 years' experience in the computer industry, Kevin Wilson has made a career out of technology and showing others how to use it. After earning a master's degree in computer science, software engineering, and multimedia systems, Kevin has held various positions in the IT industry including graphic & web design, programming, building & managing corporate networks, and IT support.

He serves as senior writer and director at Elluminet Press Ltd, he periodically teaches computer science at college, and works as an IT trainer in England while researching for his PhD. His books have become a valuable resource among the students in England, South Africa, Canada, and in the United States.

Kevin's motto is clear: "If you can't explain something simply, then you haven't understood it well enough." To that end, he has created the Exploring Tech Computing series, in which he breaks down complex technological subjects into smaller, easy-to-follow steps that students and ordinary computer users can put into practice.

0-9

100BaseFX is an Ethernet LAN standard that runs over fibre optic cable at 100Mbps and can carry data a maximum distance of 2km. "Base" indicates baseband signalling, and the letter "F" indicates fiber-optic cable.

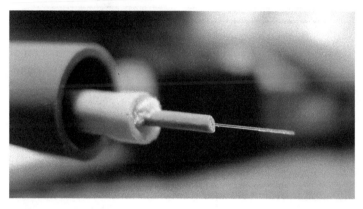

100BaseT is an Ethernet standard that runs at 100Mbps over UTP cable such as Cat5 or Cat5e, and can carry data up to 100m. "Base" indicates baseband signalling, and the letter "T" indicates twisted pair copper cabling.

1000BaseT also known as Gigabit Ethernet, is an Ethernet standard that runs at 1Gbps over UTP cable such as Cat-5e, Cat-6, or Cat-7 and can carry data up to 100m.

1080i is a display resolution used in HDTV with a resolution of 1920×1080 pixels and is also known as Full HD. The "i" stands for interlaced where the image is refreshed on the screen by scanning lines 1, 3, 5... on the first scan, then lines 2, 4, 6... on the second scan.

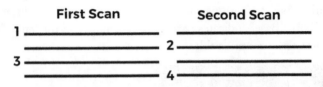

1080p is a display resolution used in HDTV with a resolution of 1920×1080 pixels and is also known as Full HD. The "p" stands for progressive scan where the image on the screen is refreshed by scanning each line in sequence.

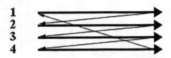

10Base2 also known as thinnet and is a variant of Ethernet that uses thin coaxial cable terminated with BNC connectors to connect computers together.

10BaseT is an Ethernet LAN standard that runs over UTP cable and runs at 10mbps.

16-Bit Audio is a unit of measure that indicates the resolution of a digitised sound sample and uses 16 bits per sample. The higher the resolution, the better the audio fidelity. 16-bit audio is the standard used for standard audio Compact Discs (CD-DA)

1GL or First Generation Language is a programming language that uses nothing but binary machine code.

24p refers to 24 frames per second progressive scan. This is the frame rate of motion picture film. It is also one of the rates allowed for transmission in the DVB and ATSC television standards, allowing them to handle film without needing any frame rate change. It is now accepted as a part of television production formats, usually associated with high-definition, 1080-line, progressive scans.

2-Factor Authentication is an extra level of security included in many online services, where a confirmation code is sent to the user's cell/mobile phone number or email address that was registered when the account was opened.

2GL or Second Generation Language is a programming language that uses assembly language mnemonics which are assembled into machine code for execution.

3D API is a 3D application programming interface that controls all aspects of the 3D rendering process such as Microsoft's DirectX and OpenGL.

3D Graphics is the display of objects and scenes in 3 dimensions: height, width, and depth. The information is calculated using 3D a co-ordinate system that represents three dimensions as x, y, and z axes.

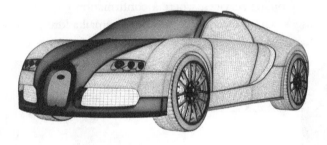

3D Sound   is a blanket term for technologies that alter the way sound is distributed in real-world space. Spatialisation broadens the soundstage (the area in space where the sound seems to be coming from), making it more dramatic and spacious, and gives the illusion of pushing it beyond the physical location of the speakers. Positional audio uses encoded audio streams to position sounds realistically in the space around the listener when the sounds are played back on compatible equipment.

3G is short for Third Generation wireless mobile telecommunications technology.

3GL or Third Generation Language is a programming language that is machine independent that uses english-like statements that are compiled or interpreted for execution. Common examples are C, C++, Python, Basic and Pascal.

4G is short for Fourth Generation wireless mobile telecommunications technology, and the successor to 3G.

4GL or Fourth Generation Language uses english like statements with a minimum of programming code such as SQL.

4K also known as UltraHD (or UHD) and is a resolution used in digital televisions and monitors with a resolution of 3840×2160 pixels in many consumer displays (2160p), and 4096×2160 in digital cinema.

5G is short for Fifth Generation wireless mobile telecommunications technology, and the successor to 4G.

68000 is a CISC microprocessor introduced in 1979 by Motorola and was used in the Apple Lisa and early models of Amiga, Atari ST, and Macintosh computers.

5GL or Fifth Generation Language is a programming language that is based on problem-solving and is often used in AI.

720i is a resolution used in HDTV with a resolution of 1280×720 pixels, and is also known as HD Ready. The "i" stands for interlaced where the image is refreshed on the screen by scanning lines 1, 3, 5 on the first scan, then lines 2, 4, 6... on the second scan.

```
        First Scan          Second Scan
1 ─────────────────    ─────────────────
                   2 ─────────────────
3 ─────────────────
                   4 ─────────────────
```

720p is a resolution used in HDTV with a resolution of 1280×720 pixels and is also known as HD Ready. The "p" stands for progressive scan where the image on the screen is refreshed by scanning each line in sequence.

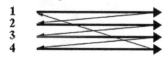

802.11a is a wireless networking standards that operates in the 5 GHz band with a maximum net data rate of 54 Mbps.

802.11ac is a wireless networking standards that operates in the 5 GHz band with a maximum net data rate of 500 Mbps - 1Gbps.

802.11b is a wireless networking standards that operates in the 2.4 GHz band with a maximum net data rate of 11 Mbps.

802.11g is a wireless networking standards that operates in the 2.4 GHz band with a maximum net data rate of 22 Mbps.

802.11n is a wireless networking standards that operates on both 2.4 and 5 GHz band with a maximum net data rate of 54 - 600 Mbps.

8086 is a 16-bit microprocessor chip designed by Intel that gave rise to the x86 architecture. The chip had a 16-bit data bus, 20-bit external bus, 64K I/O ports and ran at up to 10Mhz.

80286 an Intel 16-bit microprocessor that was introduced on February 1, 1982.

80386 an Intel 32-bit microprocessor introduced in 1985.

80486 an Intel 32-bit microprocessor introduced in 1989

8-Bit Audio is audio that is digitised using 8 bits.

AAAA Record is a record on a DNS server that maps a domain name to an IPv6 address.

A Record is a record on a DNS server that maps a domain name to the IPv4 address.

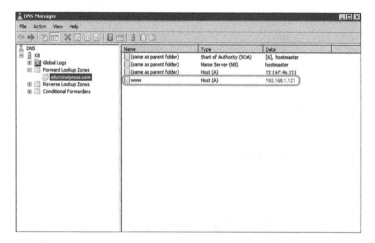

A3D is a positional audio technology and audio API developed by Aureal Semiconductor Inc. A3D provides a real-life audio experience by surrounding the listener with sounds in 3D using only a single pair of ordinary speakers or headphones.

Abort is to terminate or stop a computer program from running usually when there is an error.

AC stands for Alternating Current and is the electricity generated at a power plant and distributed to homes and offices. The voltage is 110v in the US and 250v in the UK. Alternating means the direction of the current is reversed 60 times a second (60Hz) in the US and 50 times a second (50Hz) in the UK.

AC 97 is an audio codec standard developed by Intel in 1997 used on PC motherboards and sound cards to supply audio to the system.

Access Control List is a list of permissions that specify what operations a user can perform on a resource such as a shared resource, folder or file.

Access Time is the time taken between the requested for data from memory or a peripheral device, and the moment the information is returned. Access time includes the actual seek time, rotational latency, and command processing overhead time.

Accumulator is a register in the CPU used to temporarily store the result of a calculation during the execution of an instruction.

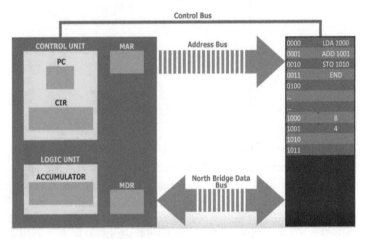

ACK short for acknowledgement, a notification sent from one network device to another to acknowledge an event or receipt of a message.

ACPI stands for Advanced Configuration and Power Interface and is an interface for controlling power management and monitoring the health of the computer system.

ACR stands for Advanced Communication Riser, a rival riser card architecture to Intel's CNR specification, which emerged at about the same time and offers similar features.

Acrobat is an Adobe application for producing documents that can either be printed or displayed on the screen, with the correct fonts and layout on a variety of different devices and operating systems. Usually a PDF document.

Action Center is a slideout panel included in Windows 10 that displays notifications from various apps, system events, and provides quick access toggles to various settings.

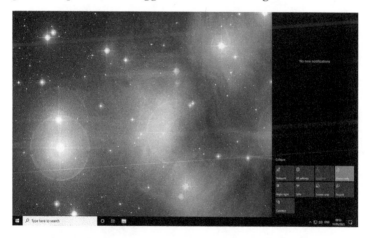

Active Directory is a directory service usually running on a server called a domain controller and is found on Microsoft Domain Networks. The active directory contains registered user accounts, as well as any available services and resources such as printers, etc

Active Matrix is an LCD technology used in flat panel monitors and televisions that produces a brighter and sharper display with a broader viewing angle than passive matrix screens. Active matrix technology uses a thin film transistor at each pixel and is often designated as a TFT screen. See also Passive Matrix.

ActiveX is a deprecated technology developed by Microsoft. Introduced in 1996, ActiveX components (or controls) were embedded in web pages to extend functionality and interactivity. Most modern browsers no longer support ActiveX.

Actuator is the internal mechanism of a hard disk drive that moves the read/write head to the correct track on the surface of the disk. The actuator itself, typically consists of a rotary voice coil and a series of arms. At the end of each arm is a read/write head. As a voltage is applied to the voice coil, it rotates, positioning the heads over the desired track on the surface of the disk.

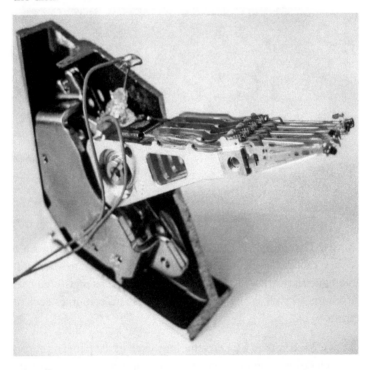

Adaptive Compression is data compression software that continually changes its compression algorithm depending on the type and content of the data being compressed.

ADC is short for analogue to digital converter and is a device that converts continuously varying analogue signals into binary code for the computer. The converter may be contained on a single chip or can be one circuit within a chip.

ADD2 is a PCI Express card that can be used to display system output on a television, digital display, or simultaneously to a monitor and digital display.

Adder or Full Adder is a digital circuit that is used in the arithmetic logic unit of a CPU to add two numbers.

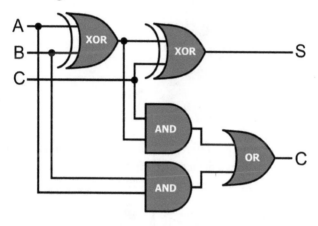

A and B are the two numbers being added together, C is the carry. The truth table would be:

Input			Output	
A	**B**	**CARRY**	**SUM**	**CARRY**
0	0	0	0	0
0	0	1	1	0
0	1	0	1	0
0	1	1	0	1
1	0	0	1	0
1	0	1	0	1
1	1	0	0	1
1	1	1	1	1

Additive Colour also known as RGB colour. Additive colours are created by mixing different amounts of light using the three primary colours: red, green, and blue. Additive colour mixing begins with black and ends with white, meaning that as more colour is added, the result is lighter and more white. TVs, projectors and computer monitors use the additive colour to create images on screen.

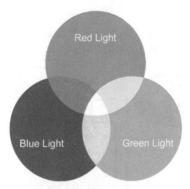

Address is a unique reference point to a memory location, a location on a storage device, or peripheral device. This is known as an absolute address or real address.

Relative address is an address expressed as an offset from the value of a register such as the program counter (PC), or the distance from a base address.

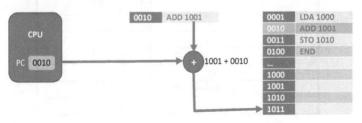

Address Bus is the channel between the CPU to the main memory (RAM) that allows the CPU to send an address to the memory controller.

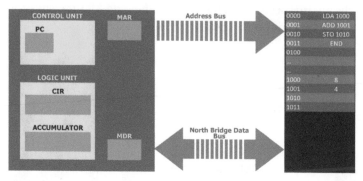

Address Space is the total amount of memory addresses the address bus can contain.

Addressability refers to how many pixels can be sent to the display horizontally and vertically. The most common combinations currently in use are 640×480 (VGA mode), 800×600 (SVGA mode), 1024×768, 1280×1024 and 1600×1200.

Administrator is a user account often created when the operating system is installed that allows full access to the system.

Administrator Tools are specialised utilities and programs used for backup, monitoring, error checking, troubleshooting and system management.

ADSL stands for Asymmetrical Digital Subscriber Line, and is a data communications technology provided over copper telephone lines. With ADSL, the download speed is greater than the upload speed, hence the name asymmetric. Max transmission speed depends on the distance from the exchange.

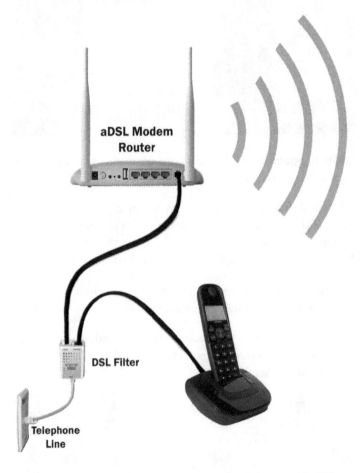

Adware is a program that tracks your activity across different websites and generates targeted adverts and popups usually to the annoyance of the user.

AGP stands for Accelerated Graphics Port and is a 32-bit PC bus architecture introduced in 1997 allowing graphics cards direct access to the system bus, rather than going through the slower PCI bus. AGP was phased out in favour of PCI-Express.

AHCI stands for Advanced Host Controller Interface defined by Intel that provides a standard interface that enables software to communicate with a SATA device such as a hard disk drive using advanced SATA features such as native command queuing (NCQ), hot swapping and power management.

AI is short for Artificial Intelligence and is the branch of computer science concerned with developing machines to perform tasks such as problem solving, learning through experience, language, and decision making. This could be applied to computer games, natural language such as Siri or Alexa, and in robotics.

AIIF stands for Audio Interchange File Format and is used for high end audio applications.

Algorithm is a sequence of instructions a computer uses to perform a task. An example could be a search algorithm that searches a database for a given term, or a sort algorithm that sorts a list into alphabetical order.

Aliasing is a form of image distortion associated with signal sampling. A common form of aliasing is a stair-stepped appearance along diagonal and curved lines. Another is moiré, two geometrically regular patterns such as two sets of parallel lines or two halftone screens superimposed.

Alpha is an additional colour component along with red, green, and blue (RGB) channels often used to denote transparency or opacity.

Alpha Blending uses the alpha channel to control how an object or bitmap interacts visually with its surroundings in computer graphics. It can be used to layer multiple textures onto a 3D object, or to simulate the translucency of glass or mask out areas of background.

Alpha Channel is the component of an image that is used to determine the transparency or opacity of a colour and is usually expressed as a percentage. Full transparency is 0% and full opacity is 100%.

ALT GR or ALT Graph Key is a modifier key on a keyboard often used to insert special characters, or international characters such as currency, accent letters or special typographic marks.

For example.

```
AltGr 4 = €
AltGr R = ®
AltGr C = ©
AltGr T = ™
```

ALT Key is a modifier key on a keyboard often used in keyboard shortcuts.

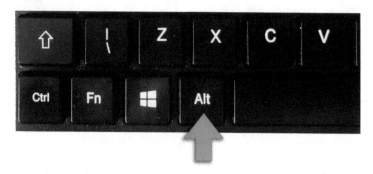

ALU is short for Arithmetic and Logic Unit: the part of a CPU that performs arithmetic commands such as addition, subtraction, multiplication and division, as well as logic commands such as OR, AND, or NOT.

AM is short for Amplitude Modulation and is a data transmission technique that encodes the data by varying (or modulating) the amplitude of the carrier wave.

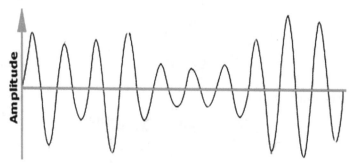

Ambient Light Sensor is an optical sensor that detects the amount of ambient light in an environment. Ambient light sensors are often found in laptops, tablets and mobile phones allowing the device to automatically control the screen's brightness

Analogue

Analogue is a signal or data that is represented by a continuously varying physical quantity such as a voltage. The signal is subject to interference from an electromagnetic source.

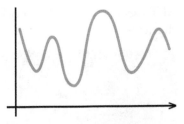

Analogue Video is a video that is represented by an analogue signal which also includes luminance, brightness (Y) and chrominance (U & V). See analogue and digital.

Anamorphic means unequally scaled in vertical and horizontal dimensions. Footage is shot with an anamorphic lens and appears squashed when captured but is correct when played back. In this way, the footage can be formatted with varying aspect ratios such as 16:9 or 4:3

AND Gate has two inputs. AND gates require both inputs to be 1 for the output to be 1. Expressed as Out = A.B

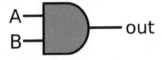

The truth table would be

A	B	Output
0	0	0
0	1	0
1	0	0
1	1	1

Android an open source mobile operating system based on a modified linux kernel found on touchscreen smartphones and tablets.

Animated GIF is a file containing a series of images commonly used on websites for short animated effects

Anode is the positively charged electrode used to attract (negatively charged) electrons in a CRT monitor.

ANSI is short for American National Standards Institute. A standards-setting, non-government organisation which develops and publishes standards for voluntary use in the United States.

Anti-aliasing is the process of smoothing out the jagged edges of bitmapped images by modulating the intensity on either side of the edge boundaries creating blurring which reduces the jagged appearance.

Anit-malware is a software utility, such as malwarebytes, designed to remove malicious programs from a computer and to prevent them from damaging a computer or data.

Apache a free open-source cross-platform web server software that powers various web servers on the internet, and is actively maintained by the Apache Software Foundation. Apache usually runs on a linux distribution but can also run on windows.

Aperture Grille is a series of thin, closely-spaced vertical wires are used to isolate pixels horizontally. The pixels are separated vertically by the nature of the scan lines used to compose the image. This is the phosphor separation method used in a Trinitron CRT in place of a shadow mask.

API is short for Application Programming Interface and is a set of functions that an application can call to perform a task. APIs allow one application to communicate with other applications and services without having to know how they're written. For example, if you're using a Windows application such as Word, and you want to save a file, Word will call the save dialog box function from the Windows API.

APM stands for Advanced Power Management and is an API that allows an OS to communicate with the computer's BIOS to reduce power consumption by throttling components or turning them off.

App is a software application often found on tablets and smartphones. Apps are usually smaller than applications and are designed to take advantage of touch screens on mobile devices

Applet is a small program that performs a limited range of tasks such as a Java applet.

Application is a piece of software or computer program written to perform a task such as Microsoft Word and Adobe Photoshop.

Architecture is a specification that describes how hardware and software technologies are designed and how they interact to form a computer system or platform such as the Von Neumann architecture.

Archive is to copy applications or data onto a storage medium for long-term storage of data.

Argument also known as a parameter, is a value often passed to a function or subroutine in computer programming.

```
def addNum(firstNum, secondNum):
        return firstNum + secondNum

print (addNum(3, 3))
```

Arithmetic Logic Unit See ALU.

Arithmetic Operator multiplication (*), division (/), addition (+), subtraction (-).

Arithmetic Shift in binary is a shift of the bits to the left or right preserving the sign bit.

Areal Density is the amount of data stored on a hard disk per square inch, and is equal to the tracks per inch multiplied by the bits per inch along each track.

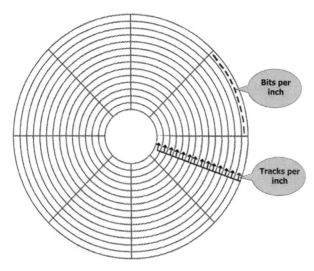

ARM is a family of high-performance RISC-based microprocessors often used in handheld devices such as PDAs tablets, some laptops and palmtops. .

ARP stands for Address resolution Protocol and is part of the TCP/IP suite used to map an IP address to the hardware MAC address.

Array is a data structure consisting of a collection of elements referenced by an index commonly used in computer programming to temporarily store data so it can be sorted or searched. Array [index]. This is a 1 dimensional array.

A 2 dimensional array has two indexes. Array [row] [col]

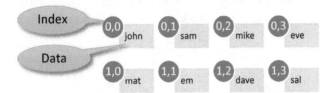

Artefact is caused by defects in compression or other digital processing. Common artefacts include jaggies, polygon shearing and pixelation.

ASCII stands for American Standard Code for Information Interchange and is a data encoding standard developed by the American National Standards Institute (ANSI) describing how characters are represented on a computer. The original ASCII character set consists of 128 7-bit characters numbered from 0 to 127 which includes numerals, punctuation marks, upper and lowercase letters of the alphabet

Char	Code	Char	Code	Char	Code	Char	Code	Char	Code	Char	Code
0	48	C	67	O	79	a	97	m	109	y	121
1	49	D	68	P	80	b	98	n	110	z	122
2	50	E	69	Q	81	c	99	o	111	Space	32
3	51	F	70	R	82	d	100	p	112	!	33
4	52	G	71	S	83	e	101	q	113	"	34
5	53	H	72	T	84	f	102	r	114	#	35
6	54	I	73	U	85	g	103	s	115	$	36
7	55	J	74	V	86	h	104	t	116	%	37
8	56	K	75	W	87	i	105	u	117	&	38
9	57	L	76	X	88	j	106	v	118	'	39
A	65	M	77	Y	89	k	107	w	119	(	40
B	66	N	78	Z	90	l	108	x	120	)	41

The ASCII character set also includes special control codes such as a carriage return or a tab.

Char	Code	Char	Code	Char	Code
NUL (null)	0	FF (NP form feed new page)	12	CAN (cancel)	24
SOH (start of heading)	1	CR (carriage return)	13	EM (end of medium)	25
STX (start of text)	2	SO (shift out)	14	SUB (substitute)	26
ETX (end of text)	3	SI (shift in)	15	ESC (escape)	27
EOT (end of transmission)	4	DLE (data link escape)	16	FS (file separator)	28
ENQ (enquiry)	5	DC1 (device control 1)	17	GS (group separator)	29
ACK (acknowledge)	6	DC2 (device control 2)	18	RS (record separator)	30
BEL (bell)	7	DC3 (device control 3)	19	US (unit separator)	31
BS (backspace)	8	DC4 (device control 4)	20		
TAB (horizontal tab)	9	NAK (negative acknowledge)	21		
LF (NL line feed new line)	10	SYN (synchronous idle)	22		
VT (vertical tab)	11	ETB (end of trans. block)	23		

Aspect Ratio is the ratio of width of an image to the height. When an image is displayed on different size screens, the aspect ratio must be kept the same to avoid stretching in either the vertical or horizontal direction. For most current monitors, this ratio 16:9.

Assembly Language is a low level programming language that uses mnemonics to represent instructions which are later assembled into machine code by and assembler. Each mnemonic such as LDA, represents a machine code instruction.

```
LDA 1000      // load ACC with value at address 1000
ADD 1001      // add value stored at address 1001
STO 1010      // store value in ACC at address 1010
END           // halt program
```

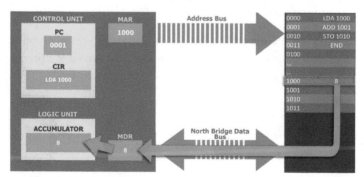

Asset a term for all the constituent media files (such as text, graphics, sounds, video) that make up a multimedia movie.

Assignment Operator is often used in computer programming to assign a value to a variable, the most common being an equals sign. There are also various other assignment operators.

Operator	Description	Example	Notes
=	Assigns values from the right side of equals sign (a+c) to the left (b)	b = a + c	assigns result of a + c to b
+=	Adds right operand (a) to the left operand (b) then assigns the result to left operand	b += a	same as b = b + a
-=	Subtracts right operand (a) from the left operand (b) then assigns the result to left operand	b -= a	same as b = b - a
*=	Multiplies right operand (a) with the left operand (b) then assigns the result to left operand	b *= a	same as b = b * a
/=	Divides left (b) operand with the right operand (a) then assigns the result to left operand	b /= a	same as b = b / a
%=	Takes modulus of the two operands then assigns the result to left operand	b %= a	same as b = b % a
**=	Performs an exponential calculation on operators then assigns value to the left operand	b **= a	same as b = b ** a
//=	Performs floor division on operators then assigns value to the left operand	b //= a	same as b = b // a

Astable an electronic device with two states used for timing in digital watches or a computer clock timing pulse. The 555 timer is an example of an astable integrated circuit.

Asymmetric Compression is a system which requires more processing capability to compress an image than to decompress an image. It is typically used for the mass distribution of programs on media such as CD-ROM, where significant expense can be incurred for the production and compression of the program but the playback system must be low in cost.

Asymmetric Encryption also known as public-key encryption is a cryptographic encryption system that uses two keys: a private key and a public key, often used in SSL certificates for HTTPS.

A message is sent using the intended recipient's public key. The recipient uses their private key to decrypt the message.

Asynchronous refers to events that are not co-ordinated with a clock signal. Devices send and ACK to verify that a block of data has been sent.

Asynchronous Cache is SRAM that does not require a clock signal to validate its control signals. About 30% lower in price and performance compared to synchronous cache.

Asynchronous Communication is the transmission of data without the use of a clock signal, where data can be transmitted intermittently rather than in a steady stream.

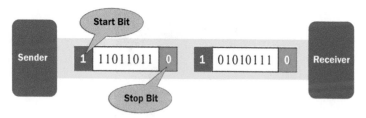

AT Bus started with the IBM-AT (Advanced Technology) systems. It is still the standard interface for most PC expansion cards. It is also known as the ISA (Industry Standard Architecture) bus.

AT Command Set was originally developed by Dennis Hayes and is the set of industry-standard commands used to control the modem. The command set consists of commands for dialing, hanging up, and changing the parameters of the connection. The vast majority of dial-up modems use the Hayes command set.

ATA stands for AT Attachment, the specification formulated in the 1980s by a consortium of hardware and software manufacturers, that defines the IDE drive interface. AT refers to the IBM PC/AT personal computer and its bus architecture.

IDE drives are sometimes referred to as ATA drives or AT bus drives. The newer ATA-2 specification defines the EIDE interface, which improves upon the IDE standard. See also IDE and EIDE.

ATAPI stands for Advanced Technology Attachment Packet Interface, a specification that defines device side characteristics for an IDE connected peripheral, such as CD-ROM or tape drives. ATAPI is essentially an adaptation of the SCSI command set to the IDE interface.

Athlon XP is the line of 7th generation AMD processors, dating from the time of the Athlon CPU's transition from the Thunderbird core to the Palomino core in 2001.

ATM stands for Asynchronous Transfer Mode: a network technology for both LANs and WANs based on transferring data in cells or packets of a fixed size that supports real-time voice and video as well as data. The topology uses a connection-oriented technique similar to the analogue telephone system, maintaining a connection for the duration of a transmission.

ATSC is an international, non-profit organisation responsible for developing voluntary standards for digital television in the USA, including the high definition television (HDTV) and standard definition television (SDTV) families of standards.

Attachment is a file such as a document or picture added to an email message.

ATX is short for **A**dvanced **T**echnology **E**xtended and is a specification used to outline motherboard and power supply configurations. ATX allows each manufacturer to put ports in a rectangular area on the back of the system. ATX power supplies produce three main outputs: 3.3v, 5v and 12v which are distributed to the motherboard using a 24 pin connector, an 8 pin auxiliary connector for the CPU and various connectors for disk drives and high end graphics cards. Shown below is a standard ATX or Full ATX board.

AU is a Unix sound file introduced by Sun Microsystems and was used on early web pages, somewhat obsolete nowadays. Also an audio file created by Audacity the free cross-platform audio editor.

Audio Card also known as a sound card, is an internal expansion card that facilitates the input and output of audio signals to and from a computer, providing the audio for multimedia applications such as music, editing video or audio, presentations, games and video projection through a speaker or sound system. Audio devices are usually connected using 1/8" (3.5mm) audio jacks.

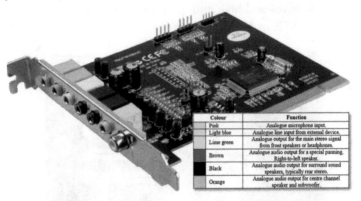

Colour	Function
Pink	Analogue microphone input.
Light blue	Analogue line input from external device.
Lime green	Analogue output for the main stereo signal from front speakers or headphones.
Brown	Analogue audio output for a special panning. Right-to-left speaker.
Black	Analogue audio output for surround sound speakers, typically rear stereo.
Orange	Analogue audio output for centre channel speaker and subwoofer.

Authoring System a software application that allows developers to design interactive courseware easily without the need for computer programming skills.

Auto Answer The modem automatically answers the phone after a certain number of rings. This is in contrast to manual answering, where a person sends an AT command to the modem to cause the modem to answer a ringing telephone.

Auto Refresh is commonly referred to as CAS before RAS refresh or CE before RE refresh. An internal address counter increments the row address each time the memory controller initiates a CAS before RAS refresh cycle.

Automatic Dialling The modem automatically dials the telephone. This is in contrast to manual dialling, where a person dials the number.

Auto-Reliable Mode The modem automatically negotiates with the remote modem for a connection, determines whether or not it can use error control and data compression during a transmission, and determines which error control and data compression protocol it can use.

Autoscan is a microprocessor-based feature of some monitors incorporating automatic synchronisation of their horizontal and vertical frequencies with those of the installed video graphics adapter. An autoscan monitor can thus operate with a wide range of video adapters.

AV short for Audio Visual or Audio Video: refers to equipment used in audio and video applications, such as microphones, videotape machines (VCRs), sound systems and hard disk systems for storing digitised audio or video data.

AV Drive or Audio Video drive is a hard disk drive that is optimised for audio and video applications. Transferring analogue high-fidelity audio and video signals onto a digital disk and playing them back at high performance levels requires a drive that can sustain continuous reads and writes without interruption. AV drives are designed to avoid thermal recalibration during reading and writing so that lengthy transfers digital video data will not be interrupted, and frames will not be lost.

Avatar is a digital representation of yourself in a digital environment.

AVC short for Advanced Video Coding also known as MPEG-4 AVC, MPEG-4 part 10 or H.264, this codec is expected to offer up to twice the compression of the current MPEG-4 ASP (Advanced Simple Profile) standard, as well as improvements in perceptual quality.

Average Seek Time is the average time it takes for the read/write head to move to a specific location. To compute the average seek time, divide the time it takes to complete a large number of random seeks by the number of seeks performed.

AVI short for Audio Video Interleaved and is Microsoft's file format for digital video and audio for Windows. AVI files contain blocks of video and audio data are interlaced together using less compression than H264 or MPEG.

AWG short for American Wire Gauge and is a standard measuring gauge for certain conductors such as copper. The higher the AWG number the thinner the wire. The origins of the gauge lie in the number of times the wire ran through a wire machine to reduce its diameter. Thus a 24-guage wire was thinner than an 18-guage wire because it ran through a wire machine 6 more times.

B

B Channel is an ISDN communication channel that carries voice, circuit or packet conversations. The B-channel is the fundamental component of ISDN interfaces. It carries 64,000 bits per seconds in either direction.

Baby AT is the form factor used by most PC motherboards in the early 1990s. The original motherboard for the PC-AT measured 12in by 13in. Baby AT motherboards are a little smaller, 8.5in by 11in.

Back Buffer is a buffer used in double-buffering. Graphics are drawn into the back buffer so that the rendering process cannot be seen by the user. When the drawing is complete, the front and back buffers are swapped.

Backdoor is a means of access to a computer system that bypasses the installed security measures often exploited by a hacker or cyber criminal.

Backlight is the light source on an LCD screen. The backlight illuminates the screen from behind the LCD panel

Backside Bus is a dedicated channel between the CPU and a Level 2 cache. The dual independent bus (DIB) architecture allows a processor to use both the backside bus and the frontside bus simultaneously.

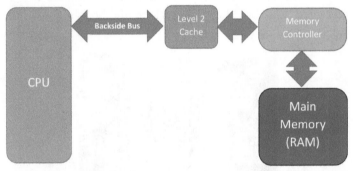

Backup is a copy of a file, directory, or volume on a separate storage device from the original, for the purpose of retrieval in case the original is accidentally erased, damaged, or destroyed. Backups can be made on tape drives, NAS drives, external hard drives to name a few. There are different types of backups. You could take a full backup which copies every single file on the system, or an incremental backup which only copies the changes since the last backup.

Backup Utility is a computer program used to create backups of data.

BACP short for Bandwidth Allocation Control Protocol and is a protocol that works in conjunction with Multilink PPP to manage bandwidth dynamically. BACP lets two devices negotiate the bandwidth as needed.

Bad Block is a block on a disk that cannot reliably hold data because of a flaw or damage.

Bad Track Table is a label affixed to the casing of a hard disk drive that tells which tracks are flawed and cannot hold data. The list is typed into the low-level formatting program when the drive is being installed.

Banding is a defect commonly found in inkjet printers that causes horizontal or vertical lines to appear on printouts usually caused by print head blockage or head misalignment.

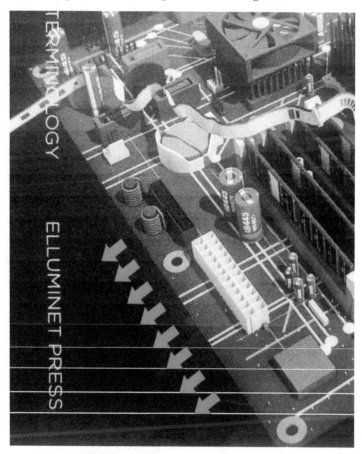

Bandwidth is the amount of data that can move through a particular interface in a given period of time, e.g. a 64-bit wide, 100 MHz SDRAM data bus has a bandwidth of 800 MBps.

Barcode is a machine readable code consisting of black vertical lines often to identify a product. The first two digits are assigned country codes or official standards agency in that country. 978 is an ISBN for a book, 0 is a US/Canadian product, 50 is UK. The rest makes up the manufacturer ID and item code. The last digit is an error check.

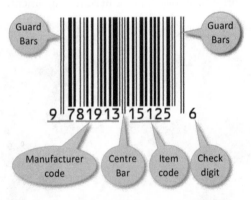

Barrel Distortion is an image distortion where the image is bowed outwards, towards the edges of the screen.

Baseband is a transmission system that only uses a single signal on the cable at a time. A common example is the Ethernet protocol, which transfers data using a baseband signal - 100BaseT.

Baud Rate is the number of symbols transmitted per second. This is not always the same as the bps rate (see also bps), because a given symbol, or baud, may have more than one bit.

BBS short for Bulletin Board System and was a site that allowed multiple users to connect to using a terminal program where they could download software, leave messages for other users, and exchange information. Bulletin Boards proliferated in the 1980s before the introduction of the world wide web. A BBS functions somewhat like a stand-alone web site with text, ASCII graphics and menu systems. Many BBSes also offered online games in which users can compete with each other.

BCC stands for Blind Carbon Copy and is used in email systems to allow the sender to send a copy of the email without the recipient knowing.

Bernoulli Drive named after a Swiss scientist who discovered the principle of aerodynamic lift. The principal characteristic of a Bernoulli drive is that the flexible disk floats between the read/write heads, so there is no actual contact, making it is less susceptible to head crashes. Iomega's zip drive used this principle.

Bezel is a name for the border around the edge of the screen. Also used to describe the rim around the edge of faceplates, and drive bays.

Bezier is a curve named after Pierre Bézier, who used the technique the 1960s for designing curves for the bodywork of Renault cars. Today bezier curves are used in graphics programs such as Adobe Illustrator.

BGA short for Ball Column Grid Array and is a specification for pin lay-outs on micro chips, such as those used on a CPU chip.

Bifringence is the property of a material which causes incident light waves of different polarisations to be refracted differently by the material.

Bi-linear Filtering improves the look of blocky, low-resolution 3D textures when viewed close up by blending and interpolating groups of texels to create a smoother image.

Binary also known as base 2, is a number system that has only two digits: 0 and 1. This number system is used in computing to encode microprocessor instructions and data.

Binary Addition. Adding two binary numbers together is fairly straight forward. All you have to remember are these simple rules...

$0 + 0 = 0$
$0 + 1 = 1$
$1 + 0 = 1$
$1 + 1 = 0$ carry 1
$1 + 1 + 1 = 1$ carry 1

Have a look at adding these two numbers together, and apply the rules quoted above.

Working from the right to the left we get:

$0+1=1, \quad 0+1=1, \quad 1+1=0$ carry 1, $\quad 1+1+0=0$ carry 1

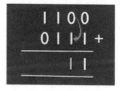

Once you work through the steps, you'll end up with something like this:

Binary Coded Decimal, or BCD for short is a coding system where each digit is represented by a fixed number of bits, usually four or eight.

21_{10} would be 0010 0001

The "2" is encoded as 0010_2 and the "1" is encoded as 0001_2

Binary Multiplication Multiplying binary numbers together is fairly straight forward. All you have to remember are these simple rules...

0 x 0 = 0
0 x 1 = 0
1 x 0 = 0
1 x 1 = 1

Lets try an example. Multiply 101 x 11
First we multiply 101 by the first 1, following the rules above.

101
__11__ x
101

Then on the next line, we put a 0 as a place-holder

101
__11__ x
101
____**0** <-- add place-holder

Then multiply 101 by second 1, which produces 101.
101
__11__ x
101
1010 +

Once you've done the that, add the two together (101 + 1010)

101
__11__ x
101
1010 +
1111

So 101 x 11 = 1111   (in decimal 5 x 3 = 15)

Binary Search is a search algorithm that repeatedly divides a sorted list into two smaller halves and discards the list that doesn't contain the value being searched for. If we search for 14. Find middle of array, check to see if 14 is greater or less than 22.

1	2	4	12	14	**22**	24	56	66	88	90
					14<22					

In this case it is less, so discard right hand side of array

1	2	**4**	12	14
		14>4		

Repeat process, this time it's greater so discard left hand side. Keep repeating until you end up with the searched value.

12	14
14>12	

14

Binary Shift is a way of multiplying or dividing binary numbers. To multiply a number by 2, shift all the digits in the binary number along to the left and fill the gaps after the shift with a 0. This is also known as a logical shift and is best used on unsigned binary numbers. To multiply by 4 shift the digits two places.

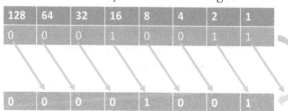

To divide shift all the binary numbers to the right.

Binary Tree is a tree data structure in which each leaf or node has at most two children, commonly used in sorting and compression algorithms such as a binary search tree or in huffman coding.

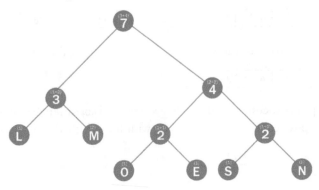

Biometric is a device often used in user authentication and works by scanning a finger print, face, or retina.

BIOS a small program stored in permanent ROM and is soldered directly onto the motherboard. BIOS Stands for Basic Input Output System and is responsible for checking hardware components at bootup, called a power on self test (POST).

BISYNC short for BInary SYNChronous: a major category of synchronous communications protocols, developed by IBM and used in mainframe networks. Bisync communications require that both sending and receiving devices are synchronised before transmission of data is started. Contrast with asynchronous transmission.

Bit is short for binary digit, and is basic unit of data storage. A bit can either be a 1 or 0. There are 8 bits in 1 byte.

Bit Depth in colour images, is the number of colours used to represent the image. Typical values are 8-, 16- and 24-bit colour, allowing 256, 65,536 and 16,777,216 colours to be represented. The latter is known as true colour, because 16.8 million different colours is about as many as the human eye can distinguish. Devices that support 32-bit colour use an 8-bit alpha channel to define a possible 256 levels of opacity. Also referred to as colour depth.

Bit/s stands for Bits Per Second and is the speed at which data travels over a communications line. For example, a modem that operates at 9600 bits per second can transfer 9600 binary digits each second. A character normally consists of eight bits, plus the start and stop bits that separate the character from other transmitted characters.

Bitmap also known as a raster image, uses thousands of pixels in varying colours and intensities to represent an image. Each pixel on screen is represented by a number of bits. Each pixel can be represented by one bit (simple black and white) or up to 32 bits (high-definition colour). A raw image bitmap commonly uses the file extension "bmp". Many image file formats use compressed bitmap variants, often with additional meta-data such as GIF, JPEG, EXIF, PNG, and TIFF.

Bleeding is a print distortion where adjacent colours run or merge into one another usually caused by excess ink or paper which is too absorbent.

Block Data is organised into logical "blocks" for transmission between devices. Blocks may be fixed or variable length, with block sizes of 512 or 1024 bytes being particularly common. An example of a block format is: preamble, user data, CRC, postamble.

Blockiness is the consequence of portions of an image breaking into little squares due to over-compression or a video file overwhelming a computer's processor. See also Artefact.

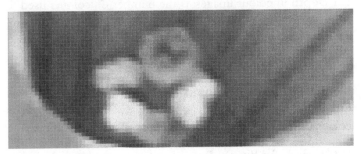

Blooming is a problem where bright white areas have a slight halo around them.

BLT stands for Bit-aLigned Block Transfer and is the process of copying pixels or other data from one place in memory to another.

Bluetooth is a wireless technology for exchanging data over short distances using a frequency of 2.4 to 2.485 GHz. This is often referred to as a PAN (or personal areal network) and can be used to connect headphones, wireless mice, smart phones and make small data transfers.

Bluray is an optical storage medium used to store digital data such as computer files, software, videos and high definition films (720p and 1080p). They look very similar to DVDs except they have a greater storage capacity. Single-layer blurays can store up to 25GB. Dual layer discs can store up to 50GB.

BNC is a connector used for composite video on commercial video devices.

Was also used as a video connection type consisting of five separate cables for red, green, blue, and horizontal/vertical synchronisation signals on high end monitors.

BNF stands for Backus–Naur form and is often used to describe the syntax of programming languages, communication protocols, instruction sets and document formats. For example:

`<postal-address> ::= <name> <street> <code>`

Meaning a postal address consists of a name, followed by a street name, then a zip/post code.

Boolean Logic Named after the nineteenth-century mathematician George Boole, Boolean logic is a branch of algebra used for evaluating true/false statements using the operators AND, OR, NOT, NAND, NOR, XOR.. Boolean Logic is often used to evaluate logic gates when building electronic circuits.

Boot Drive The drive that the operating system first loads from (usually labelled "C" on a Windows machine).

Boot Sector is a reserved sector on a disk that is used to load the operating system. On start-up, the computer looks for the master book record (MBR) which is typically the first sector in the first partition of the disk. The MBR points to the first sector of the partition that contains the operating system (derived from the phrase "pulling yourself up from your bootstraps").

Bootloader is the program responsible for loading the operating system.

Bot or internet bot is a program that runs automated tasks on the internet.

BPI stands for Bits Per Inch and is a measure of how densely information is packed on a storage medium. See also Flux Density.

BPP stands for Bits Per Pixel and is the number of bits used to represent the colour value of each pixel in a digitised image.

bps is short for Bits Per Second and is the speed at which data is transferred to and from a storage medium or over a network. Note lowercase "b" indicates bits.

Bps is short for Bytes per second. Capital "B" indicates bytes. The speed at which data is transferred to and from a storage medium or over a network.

BRI stands for Basic-Rate Interface and is the basic ISDN setup, consisting of two 64 Kbit/s B-channels (bearer channels), which carry data and voice in both directions, and one 16 Kbit/s D-channel, which carries call- control information. See also PRI.

Bridge is a device that operates at the data link layer (Layer 2) of the OSI 7 layer model and whose function is to connect and pass packets of information between two networks.

Brightness is a measure of the overall intensity of an image.

The lower the brightness value, the darker the image. The higher the value, the lighter the image.

Broadband is the name given to any fast, permanent internet connection delivered by cable, satellite, mobile, fibre optics and ADSL.

Also any communications channel that transmits multiple data signals at the same time. Contrast with Baseband.

BTX stands for Balanced Technology Extended and is Intel's interface specification developed as an evolutionary follow-on to the ATX form factor and designed to better accommodate modern-day PC technologies and lead to cooler, quieter, and more efficient PCs of all sizes.

Bubble Jet is Canon's trade name for its thermal drop on demand inkjet printer technology. The ink is heated, which produces a bubble that expands and ejects the ink out of the nozzle. As the bubble cools, the vacuum created draws fresh ink back into the nozzle.

Bubble Sort compares all the element one by one and sort them based on their values. Take the list:

```
21, 6, 2, 15
```

If we want to bubble sort this list into ascending order, we start by comparing the first number with the second number.

```
21
        Compare. If first number > second number, swap
6

2
```

If the first number is greater than the second number, we swap the numbers.

```
6
        Swap
21

2
```

Repeat the process with the second, third, and forth element, until you get to the end of the list. Then we go through the list again and repeat the process. You'll need to go through the list as many times as it takes until they're all in order.

So once complete, you'll end up with:

```
2, 6, 15, 21
```

This type of sort is inefficient.

Buffer sometimes known as a cache is a location used for temporary storing data that is read from or waiting to be written to another device. A buffer is used to speed up access to many devices such as a hard disk.

Bug is an error in a computer program that causes erratic in correct results or a crash.

Bump Mapping in computer graphics is a 3D lighting technique designed to give a texture a three-dimensional, animated feel.

Burn is the process of writing data to a writable optical disk such as a DVD-R or CD-R

Burst Mode a rapid data-transfer technique that automatically generates a block of data (a series of consecutive addresses) every time the processor requests a single address. The assumption is that the next data-address the processor will request will be sequential to the previous one. Burst mode can be applied to both read operations (from memory) and write operations (to memory).

Burst Transfer Rate is the maximum amount of data per second a drive can supply intermittently; this is limited by the disk interface and is typically 16.6 MBps (using PIO Mode 4).

Bus is a connection between components inside a computer. The connection is made up of a set of wires called lines that can only carry 1 bit at a time. So a bus can have 32 or 64 different lines, hence we get 32 bit buses and 64 bit buses. There are many different kinds of bus including data bus, address bus, control bus, ISA, EISA, MCA, and the PCI-Express bus.

Bus Master IDE is the capability of a drive to effect data transfers from disk to memory with minimum intervention by the CPU known as Direct Memory Access (DMA) transfers.

Bus Topology is a network configuration in which all the devices are connected to a single cable called a bus

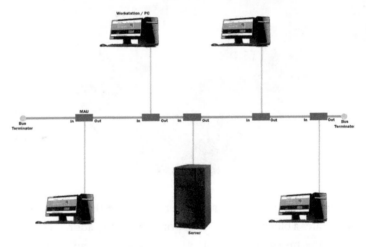

Byte is a unit of digital storage consisting of eight bits. A character on a computer system can be represented by one byte of data.

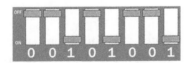

C

C is a general-purpose, procedural computer programming language developed at Bell Labs by Dennis Ritchie.

C++ is a general-purpose high level object oriented programming language created by Bjarne Stroustrup as an extension of the C programming language

Cable Modem is a modem that uses part of the capacity of the local cable system to transmit data rather than TV channels to the home. It works much like a Local Area Network. Unlike the typical cable system, where TV signals can only be broadcast to the home, information is allowed to be transmitted in both directions.

Cache is an intermediate storage capacity between the processor and the RAM or disk drive. The most commonly used instructions are held here, allowing for faster processing.

Cache Buffer is an intermediate storage capacity between the processor and the disk drive used to store data likely to be requested next. Also known as Data Buffer. See also Look Ahead.

Cache Controller is the circuit that controls the interface between the CPU, cache and main memory (RAM) .

Cache Hit is when the address requested by the CPU is found in cache. Conversely, cache miss is when it's not found.

Cache Memory is a small block of high-speed memory (usually SRAM) located between the CPU and main memory that is used to store frequently requested data and instructions. Properly designed, a cache improves system performance by reducing the need to access the system's slower main memory for every transaction.

Camera an optical device used to capture an image. In 3D graphics, the viewpoint through which a scene is viewed. Flythroughs of scenes are conceptually a moving camera.

Candela is a unit of measurement of the intensity of light. An ordinary wax candle generates one candela. The maximum brightness for CRTs is about 100 to 120 cd/m2 and for TFTs, up to 250 cd/m2.

CAP short for Carrierless Amplitude Phase and is a multilevel multiphase encoding method used with ADSL technology. CAP uses frequency modulation techniques for sending signals over standard copper twisted-copper wire, giving data bit combinations a form of both amplitude and phase. Unlike DMT, CAP uses the whole frequency range from 4KHz up to 1.1MHz as a single channel. It is used in the V.32/V.32bis modem communication standard.

Capacitor is an electronic component that holds a charge.

Capacity is the amount of data that can be stored on a storage device. Capacity is usually expressed in megabytes, gigabytes or terabytes depending on the size.

Captcha is a test that includes an image of distorted text used to determine whether a user is human or an automated bot. These captcha tests are usually included in online forms or account sign in pages. The user must decipher the text and enter it into the field.

Carrier is the base signal used to transmit data across a telephone line. The modem modulates this signal (alters its frequency or phase) to encode the data to be transmitted.

CAS short for Column Address Select (or Strobe) and is a control pin on a DRAM memory module used to latch and activate a column address. The column selected on a DRAM module is determined by the data present at the address pins when CAS becomes active. Used with RAS and a row-address to select a bit within the DRAM.

CAT5 is a standardized twisted pair cable for connecting devices such as computers, routers and switches to an ethernet network. CAT5 is suitable for fast ethernet (100BaseT) or gigabit ethernet (1000BaseT), and has a limit of about 100m. The cables are terminated with a standard RJ45 connector. Here is the pinout for the T568B wiring specification.

Catalina is the sixteenth major release of macOS for Macintosh computers. Catalina introduced a feature called sidecar which allows you to extend your Mac's desktop onto an iPad.

Cathode is an electrode that is negatively charged. Electrons are released from the cathode in a CRT monitor.

CCIA stands for Computer and Communications Industry Association and is a trade association composed of computer and communications firms. It represents their interests in domestic and foreign trade, and keeps members advised of relevant standards and regulatory policy.

CCIR is short for Consultative Committee for International Radio communications.

CCIR 601 is a recommendation developed by the International Radio Consultative Committee for the digitisation of colour video signals. The CCIR 601 recommendation deals with colour space conversion from RGB to VCrCb, the digital filters used for limiting the bandwidth, the sample rate (defined as 13.5 MHz), and the horizontal resolution (720 active pixels).

CCITT short for Consultative Committee for International Telephone and Telegraph and is an international standards organisation dedicated to creating communications protocols that will enable global compatibility for the transmission of voice, data, and video across all computing and telecommunications equipment. Changed its name to the International Telecommunications Union (ITU) in 1993.

CDMA stands for Code Division with Multiple Access and is a technology for digital transmission of radio signals that uses digital encoding and spread spectrum RF techniques to allow multiple users to share the same RF channel. In CDMA, a frequency is divided using codes, rather than time or frequency.

CDPD Cellular Digital Packet Data: a wireless communications protocol – widely used by law enforcement agencies – which enables users to transmit packets of data over the cellular network using a portable computing device and a CDPD modem.

CDTV Commodore Dynamic Total Vision: consumer multimedia system from Commodore that includes CD-ROM/CD audio player, Motorola 68000 processor, 1MB RAM, and 10-key infrared remote control.

CeBIT A computer exhibition hosted in Hannover, Germany in the spring of each year. The exhibition is a spin-off from the more broadly-based Hannover Fair trade show and debuted in 1986.

Cellular Network or mobile network is a wireless network distributed over land which is divided into areas called cells.

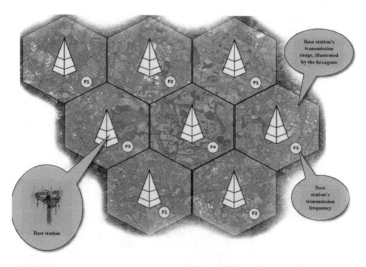

This is how a cell phone or mobile phone network operates. Each of these cells is assigned a frequency (eg F1-F4) each served by a radio base station. The frequencies can be reused in other cells, provided that the same frequencies are not reused in neighbouring cells as it would cause interference.

CELP short for Card Edge Low Profile and is a socket often used for cache modules.

Centronics Interface also known as a parallel port is a 36-pin connection designed by Centronics Corporation and was used to connect a printer to a computer. Somewhat obsolete nowadays.

CGA is a low-resolution video display standard, invented for the first IBM PC. CGA's highest resolution mode is 2 colours at a resolution of 640 x 200 pixels.

CGI (graphics) Short for Computer Generated Imagery. The use of 3D modelling to create characters, objects and environments for use in films and television programs, videos, or computer games.

CGI (web) Common Gateway Interface: a standard method of extending Web server functionality by executing programs or scripts on a Web server in response to Web browser requests. A common use of CGI is in form processing, where the browser sends the form data to a CGI script on the server, and the script integrates the data with a database and sends back a results page as HTML.

CGM short for Computer Graphics Metafile and is a standard format that allows for graphics images.

CGMS short for Copy Guard Management System and is a method of preventing copies or controlling the number of sequential copies allowed.

CGMS/A is added to an analogue signal (such as line 21 of NTSC).

CGMS/D is added to a digital signal, such as IEEE 1394.

Chapter is a subdivisions of a video title (e.g. movie) on a DVD-Video disc, each chapter being a scene or other section as defined during authoring.

Character is a unit of information such as a letter of the alphabet, numeric digit, or punctuation symbol.

Character Recognition is the process of scanning typed or handwritten text into machine encoded characters

Character Set is a complete list of characters that are recognised by a computer such as ASCII or Unicode.

Check bit or parity bit is an extra data bit added to a string or binary code used to check for errors in an electronic transmission or data storage.

Chipset is the electronic component mounted on a motherboard that manages the flow of data between the processor, memory and other peripherals.

Chorus is a doubling effect used to enhance sound.

Chroma is the colour portion of a video signal that includes hue and saturation information. Requires luminance, or light intensity, to make it visible. Also referred to as Chrominance.

Chrome Google Chrome is a freely available web browser developed by Google and is available for Windows, Mac, Linux, iOS, Android and Chromebook.

ChromeBook is a tablet or laptop style computer running the ChromeOS operating system.

ChromeOS is a linux based operating system developed by Google for the Chromebook. ChromeOS supports both android apps from the google play store, and linux apps.

CIDR Stands for Classless Inter-Domain Routing and is an alternative IP addressing scheme that allows a more efficient allocation of IP addresses than the class based method.

CIDR notation	Netmask notation	Available hosts	Notes
/0	0.0.0.0	4,294,967,294	Max hosts with IPv4
/8	255.0.0.0	16,777,214	Class A
/16	255.255.0.0	65,533	Class B
/24	255.255.255.0	254	Class C
/25	255.255.255.128	126	
/26	255.255.255.192	62	
/27	255.255.255.224	30	
/28	255.255.255.240	14	
/29	255.255.255.248	6	
/30	255.255.255.252	2	

For example, the class C IP address 192.168.1.1 could be associated with the subnet mask of 255.255.255.0.

Meaning 192.168.1 represent the network, and the last digit represents the host. You'd express this as 192.168.1.1/24 using the CIDR notation. It means the first 24 bits of the IP address represent the network.

CIE stands for Commission International de l'Eclairage: the international organisation that establishes methods for measuring colour. Their colour standards for colourmetric measurements are internationally accepted specifications that define colour values mathematically.

CIELAB (L*a*b*) is a colour model to approximate human vision. The model consists of three variables: L* for luminosity, a* for one colour axis, and b* for the other colour axis. CIELAB is a good model of the Munsell colour system and human vision.

CIELUV (L*u*v) is a colour space model produced in 1978 by the CIE at the same time as the L*a*b model. CIE L*u*v is used with colour monitors, whereas CIE L*a*b is used with colour print production.

CIF stands for Common Interchange Format and is a standard format for picture resolution, frame rate, and the colour space of digital video.

Circuit Switching is a transmission method used to send a message over a dedicated physical path between the sender and receiver. Contrast with packet switching.

CISC stands for Complex Instruction Set Computer. This architecture uses complex instructions, meaning a single instruction can execute several operations such as a load data from memory, perform an operation, and store result in memory.

```
ADD 1000, 1001
```

Most modern computers such as PCs, Macs, and Laptops use the CISC architecture.

Clean Room An environmentally controlled dust-free assembly or repair facility in which hard disk drives are assembled or can be opened for internal servicing.

Clear To Send CTS is an RS-232C signal that tells the computer it can start sending information. See also Request To Send (RTS).

CLI stands for Command Line Interface and is a text-based interface where the user types in various commands to execute tasks or run programs. Examples include MS-DOS Command Prompt, Windows PowerShell, MacOS Terminal, and Linux Terminal.

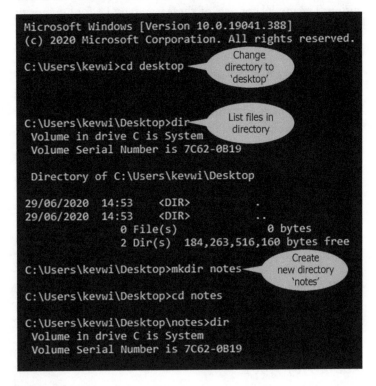

Client is any computer, device or program that uses the services of another program, computer or server..

Client-Server is a network architecture in which each computer or process on the network is either a "client" or a "server". Servers are powerful computers or processes dedicated to managing disk drives (file servers), printers (print servers), or network traffic (network servers). Clients are typically PCs or workstations on which users run applications. Contrast Peer-to-peer.

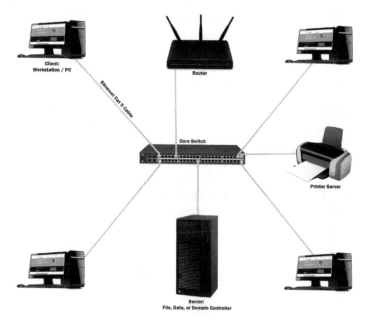

Clip Art is a library of icons, buttons, and other pre-made images that can be inserted into documents.

Clipping in audio production is the distortion that occurs when an audio signal is boosted beyond its capacity.

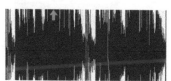

Clock is a microchip or crystal that generates a regular pulse to coordinate the functions and timing in a computer system.

Clock Doubling boosts CPU performance by increasing the internal CPU clock, while maintaining the same I/O speed (for compatibility).

Clock Rate is the number of pulses emitted from a computer's clock in one second; it determines the rate at which logical or arithmetic gating is performed in a synchronous computer.

Clock Speed is the speed at which the CPU executes instructions, usually measured in GHz.

Clone is any computer system compatible with the IBM PC standard.

Cloud is a service where data is stored remotely on servers managed and maintained by a cloud storage provider such as Dropbox, OneDrive or GoogleDrive. You connect to these services from your computer and save files to the cloud service rather than to your local machine.

Cluster is a group of sectors on a hard disk drive that is addressed as one logical unit by the operating system.

CMD or the Command Key is a modifier key on a Mac used in some keyboard shortcuts. Equivalent to the CTRL key on a PC.

CMOS stands for Complementary Metal Oxide Semiconductor: a process that uses both N- and P-channel devices in a complimentary fashion to achieve small geometries and low power consumption. CMOS is commonly used on PC motherboards and is a battery powered chip that stores the BIOS settings and hardware configuration information as well as the current time and date. The chip itself is either a separate microchip mounted on the motherboard or build into the south bridge. A CR 2032 3V coin shaped battery is often mounted on a computer's motherboard to power the CMOS RAM.

CMOS RAM is Complementary Metal Oxide Semiconductor Random Access Memory: a bank of memory that stores a PC's BIOS configuration information, including type identifiers for the drives installed in the PC, and the amount of RAM present. It also maintains the correct date, time and hard drive information for the system.

CMY is a cheaper, single cartridge inkjet that uses the Cyan Magenta Yellow model. Black here is referred to as composite black and is made up from the three colours. Dye-sublimation uses these three colours on the print ribbon.

CMYK Cyan, Magenta, Yellow, Black: the four process colours that are used in four-colour printed reproduction. By overlaying or dithering combinations of these four inks in different proportions, a vast range of colours can be created.

CNAME Record Short for Canonical Name, is a record on a DNS server used to create an alias and is commonly used to map a subdomain to a domain. Eg to map elluminetpress.com to www.elluminetpress.com, or create a subdomain such as mail.elluminetpress.com or store.elluminetpress.com

Records

Type	Name	Value	TTL	
A	elluminetpress.com	63.63.202.63	1 Hour	✏
CNAME	www	elluminetpress.com	1 Hour	✏

CO stands for Central Office, a facility that serves local telephone subscribers. In the CO, subscribers' lines are joined to switching equipment that allows them to connect to each other for both local and long distance calls.

COAST stands for Cache On A Stick and was a popular design specification for plug in L2 cache modules.

Coaxial Cable is cable consisting of a hollow outer cylindrical conductor that surrounds a single inner wire conductor. Two types of coaxial cable are currently used in LANs: 50-ohm cable, which is used for digital signalling, and 75-ohm cable, which is used for analogue signalling and high-speed digital signalling.

Codec is short for COmpression-DECompression, and is an algorithm used to compresses and decompresses video or audio data to conserve bandwidth on a transmission medium such as the internet, and for storage on a disk drive. H264, QuickTime and Video for Windows are examples.

Collision is a situation that occurs when two or more devices attempt to send a signal along the same channel at the same time. The result of a collision is generally a garbled message. All computer networks require some sort of mechanism to either prevent collisions altogether or to recover from collisions when they do occur.

Colour Balance is the process of matching the amplitudes of red, green and blue signals so the resulting mixture makes an accurate white colour.

Colour Cycling is a means of simulating motion in a video by changing colours.

Colour Keying is to superimpose one image over another for special effects. For example in movie production, subjects are usually shot against a blue or green screen allowing the editor to remove the blue/green colour and replace it with a computer generated background or scene.

Colour Palette also called a colour lookup table (CLUT), index map, or colour map, it is a commonly-used method for saving file space when creating colour images. Instead of each pixel containing its own RGB values, which would require 24 bits, each pixel holds an 8- bit value, which is an index number into the colour palette. The colour palette contains a 256-colour subset of the 16 million unique displayable colours.

Colour Temperature defines the whiteness of the white on the screen. Variations are measured in degrees Kelvin. Natural colours used in life-like images, such as people or landscapes, look more true to life when displayed at a colour temperature of 6500K. Black text on a white page is better represented by a colour temperature of 9300K.

Column is part of a memory array. A bit can be stored where a column and a row intersect.

COM Port is a connector that allow serial devices   such as serial printers, modems, or mice to be connected to PC. Communication ports are also called serial ports. To keep track of the devices, the operating system assigns names such as such as COM1, COM2 etc.

Command is an instruction given to a computer. Also a key on a mMac called the Command Key and is used in some keyboard shortcuts.

Command Line Interface A command line interface (or CLI) is a text-based interface where the user types in various commands to execute tasks or run programs. Examples include MS-DOS Command Prompt, Windows PowerShell, MacOS Terminal, and Linux Terminal.

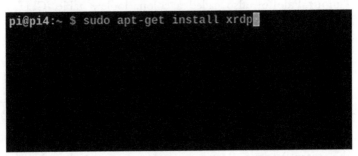

Command Mode is one of the two operating modes of the modem, sometimes called local mode or terminal mode. In command mode, the modem interprets any information it receives from the local computer (or terminal) as modem commands. It tries to perform the commands sent to it, and it returns result codes indicating the results of the commands. See also On-Line Mode.

Command Prompt is a command-line interpreter available in most operating systems such as Windows, MacOS, Unix, and Linux, where a user can enter commands to execute various tasks.

CompactFlash or CF for short is a flash memory format introduced by SanDisk Corporation in 1994 widely used for digital devices and cameras.

Compact Disc is an optical storage medium developed by Sony and Phillips to store digital recordings and computer data.

The surface of the disc is marked with pits. This is how the data is encoded onto the disc. Each time a pit is encountered, the laser beam is not reflected and is interpreted as a 0. If there is no pit, the laser beam is reflected and is interpreted as a 1.

Here we can see the inside of a CD drive.

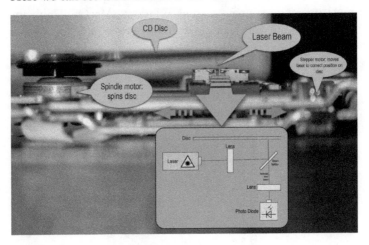

Comparison Operator is an operator often used in computer programming to compare two values.

Greater than	Greater than or equal to	Less than	Less than or equal to	Equal to
>	>=	<	<=	==

Compiler is a translation program that converts code written in a high level language such as C or C++ into machine code for execution on a computer.

Component Video carries a video signal (no audio) that has been split into three component channels: red, green, blue. It is often used to connect high end dvd players to televisions.

Composite Black is the colour back created from mixing cyan, magenta and yellow inks. Mixing inks is not a perfect operation, and composite black is often muddy. This is why the CMYK model is used in professional printing. See also True Black.

Composite Video is a video signal format that includes the complete visual waveform, including: chrominance (colour), luminance (brightness), blanking pedestal, field, line, colour sync pulses and field equalising pulses.

Compression is the encoding of data (video, audio, digital, or a combination) using a compression algorithm to reduce the amount of data for transmission or storage.

Contone is short for continuous tone and is a technique used by colour printing technologies where each colour in the image is reproduced as a single tone. See Halftone

Contrast is the range between the lightest tones and the darkest tones in an image. The lower the number value, the more closely the shades will resemble each other. The higher the number, the more the shades will stand out from each other.

Control Unit is the component of a CPU that directs the operation of the processor as it executes instructions and creates control signals that tell the Arithmetic Logic Unit (ALU) and the Registers how to operate, what to operate on, and what to do with the result. The Control Unit makes sure everything happens in the right place at the right time.

Controller is the chip that translates computer data and instructions into a form suitable for use by a device such as a hard disk controller on an hard disk drive.

Controller Card is an expansion card that interprets the commands between the processor and the disk drive.

Convergence is the term used to describe how accurately the three (red, green, and blue) electron beams converge to illuminate their respective phosphors in a colour monitor.

Cookie is a small text file created by a website that is used to store the visiting user's preferences, location, and authenticate their session in order to tailor the experience to the user, or to track the user's use of the website. Session cookies are often used to track your movements such as the contents of your basket on an e-commerce site. Persistent cookies track your preferences on the website such as locale or language. Third party cookies collect data on your online movements, eg: what sites you've been on, or what you've been searching for, usually for the purpose of advertising.

CPPM is short for Content Copy Protection for Pre-recorded Media and was a digital copy protection system used for DVD-Audio discs. Developed when the intended CSS-II method of DVD-Audio encryption was abandoned after the emergence of the DeCSS hack.

CPRM is short for Content Protection for Recordable Media and was copy protection for writeable DVD formats that ensures the contents of the discs can't be copied.

CPU stands for Central Processing Unit and is a microprocessor chip that executes the instructions of a computer program. The AMD Phenom II and Intel Core i5 are examples of a CPU. The term sometimes also refers to the case that houses this chip. See also FPU.

CRC is short for Cyclic Redundancy Check and is a mathematical error checking technique where blocks of data get a short check value attached, commonly used in computer networks and storage devices.

Crossover Cable is a UTP cable usually used to connect network devices together directly. A commonly found version of this is called a half crossed cable, where the send/receive pairs are reversed on the other end.

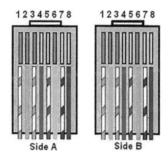

Cryptography is the process of converting ordinary plain text (called plaintext) into unintelligible text (called a cyper).

Crosstalk is interference from adjacent electronic circuitry or wire.

CRT is short for Cathode Ray Tube and is the large glass tube that made up older televisions or monitors in which rays of electrons were beamed onto a phosphorescent screen to produce images. Often still used as a generic term for a computer monitor.

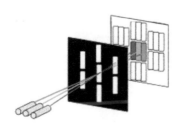

CSMA/CA Stands for Carrier Sense Multiple Access with Collision Avoidance and is a media access control protocol used on wireless networks that regulates data transmission over a shared channel. The sending host checks to see if the airway is free before sending. If the airway is free, the sending host sends a request to send signal (RTS). If there is no response to the RTS, then this means the receiving host is busy, so the sending host waits a random amount of time before trying again. If the sending host receives a clear to send signal (CTS), then it transmit its data.

CSMA/CD is short for Carrier Sense Multiple Access with Collision Detection and is a media access control protocol used in Ethernet technology for local area networking. The sending host checks to see if the line is free before sending. If the line is free, the sending host starts transmitting . If the line is not free then the sending host waits a random amount of time before trying again.

CSTN stands for Colour Super-Twist Nematic and is a passive matrix LCD technology developed by Sharp Electronics.

CTRL Key is a modifier key found on a keyboard used to execute keyboard shortcuts.

For example:
```
CTRL C = Copy
CTRL X = Cut
CTRL V = Paste
```

Cybernetics is the science of control and communication in humans and machines

Cybersecurity is the practice of protecting users, computer systems and networks from data theft, or an attack known as a cyber attack. These attacks are usually designed to access, steal or destroy information, or to extort money from users or businesses using various techniques such as phishing, malware, ransomware or social engineering.

Cyberspace is a virtual computer world that allows users to communicate, share information, play games, and engage in social media.

Cylinder is a collection of tracks on multiple surfaces that are located at the same radius on each disk surface (ie concentric tracks).

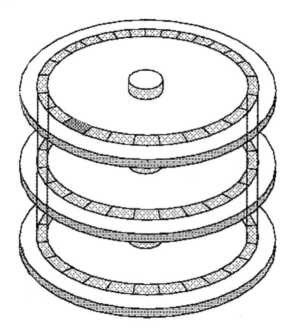

D

DAC stands for Digital-to-Analogue Converter and is a device (usually a single chip) that converts digital data into analogue signals. Graphics cards have traditionally required DACs to convert digital data to analogue signals that a monitor can process. Modems require a DAC to convert data to analogue signals that can be carried by telephone wires.

Database is an structured and organised collection of data. A common type is a relational database which is made up of tables with rows (records) containing fields of data indexed by a unique primary key. The database is searched or queried using a language called Structured Query Language. See DBMS, SQL.

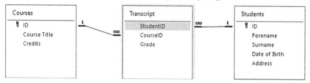

Data Bus is often used to transfer data to and from different components of a computer. This could be between the CPU and main memory or to another peripheral. The first standard for data bus was 32-bit, whereas newer systems are 64-bit.

Data Cache is a temporary data store implemented using extremely fast RAM or on a disk drive that is used to store data so that subsequent requests for the data are served faster.

Data Compression is the encoding of text or data so that it takes up less space. Data compression allows more data to be stored on a disk to save space and is also used in data transmission so more data can be transmitted in a shorter period of time and thus increases its throughput. The data is decompressed by the receiver.

Daughter Board is a printed circuit board that plugs into another larger circuit board such as a motherboard to extend its functionality.

DBMS is short for Database Management System is a piece of software that interacts with a user to capture and analyse data stored in a database. Examples include Microsoft Access, MySQL, Oracle.

DC is short for direct current and is an electrical current that travels in one direction often used to power a computer's electronic circuitry. Contrast with AC.

DCE is short for Data Circuit-terminating Equipment and is a device used to connect two DTEs over a network. Eg a modem.

D-Channel is an ISDN communication channel used for sending information between the ISDN equipment and the ISDN central office switch. The D-channel can also carry "user" packet data at rates up to 9.6 Kilobits.

DCT stands for Discrete Cosine Transform and is a coding methodology used in JPEG and MPEG image compression algorithms to reduce the number of bits for actual data compression. DCT converts data into sets of frequencies, the first being the most important. Latter frequencies are stripped away based on allowable resolution loss.

DDC stands for Display Data Channel. DDC 1/2B and 2AB are standardised techniques by which monitors and graphics cards communicate with each other to help establish the best resolution and refresh rate combination. DDC is only possible through a D-SUB connection.

DDE stands for Dynamic Data Exchange and is a system used in Windows to transfer data between two applications or two instances of the same application. DDE is also used to support OLE. See also OLE.

DDR stands for Double Data Rate and is a memory technology that works by allowing operations to occur on both the rising and falling edge of the clock cycle, thereby effectively doubling the data rate without increasing the clock frequency.

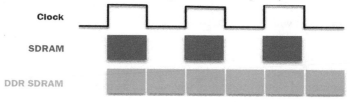

Deadlock in the context of an operating system is a situation where a resource required by a process is being held by another process, and vice versa.

Debug is the process of removing bugs or errors from a computer program.

Debugger is a development tool that allows a programmer to step through lines of code of a computer program in order to test and correct errors.

Decal is a texture that is placed specifically on one part of a 3D object.

Decimal or base 10 is the numbering system that uses 0, 1, 2, 3, 4, 5, 6, 7, 8, and 9.

Decode Unit decodes or translates complex machine language instructions into a simple format understood by the Arithmetic Logic Unit (ALU) and the Registers.

Decompression is to reverse the process used by the compression software algorithm to return data to its original size and condition.

DeCSS was an open-source Linux code that appeared in late 1990s that allowed encrypted DVD movies to be read.

Default is a predefined function or selection that is automatically selected by the computer unless the user specifies something else.

Default Gateway is the IP address of the router that connects a LAN to a wider network such as the internet. The IP address of the default gateway router is used to configure TCP/IP settings on machines connected to the LAN.

Defect Management is a technique ensuring long-term data integrity. Defect management consists of scanning disk drives both at the factory and during regular use, deallocating defective sectors before purchase and compensating for new defective sectors afterward.

Deflection Yoke is the arrangement of electromagnets which can alter the direction of the electron beam that passes through it.

Degauss in CRT monitors is the removal of the magnetic interference caused by a change in the position of the monitor in relation to the earth's magnetic field, or the presence of an artificial magnetic field that causes discolouration.

Delimiter is a character such as a comma(,) used to separate elements of data.

`Date,Name,Amount,Description`

Delta Frame also called difference frame is the frame in a video that contains only the pixels that are different from the preceding keyframe. Delta Frames reduce the overall size of the video clip to be stored on disk. See also Keyframe.

Denary is another word for decimal or base 10.

Density is a measure of how much substance there is in a given amount of space. Density = Mass divided by Volume.

Desktop Publishing or DTP for short is software such as Microsoft Publisher used to create print projects from business cards and flyers to magazines, books and posters. Many home DTP systems are affordable and designed to aid amateur level productions of common home printing tasks. More advanced DTP software packages such as Quark and InDesign are highly expensive and aimed at professional print designers.

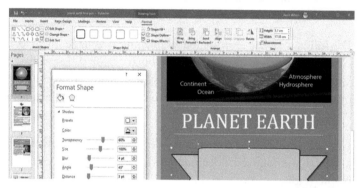

Device Driver is software often installed on an operating system that operates or controls a device such as a printer or video card, by providing a software interface to the hardware.

DHCP stands for Dynamic Host Configuration Protocol and is responsible for automatically allocating IP addresses to devices on a network. Devices connecting to a network broadcast a request to the DHCP server. The DHCP server sends back an IP address from its address pool along with a time period for which the allocation is valid called a lease, as well as DNS and gateway addresses, and the network's subnet mask.

DIB stands for Device-Independent Bitmap Format and was a common image format for Windows applications.

Die is an area of silicon containing an integrated circuit. A die has multiple layers, each with a specific function. A die refers to a semiconductor component or part that has not yet been packaged. The popular term for a die is chip.

Dielectric is a substance that is a poor conductor of electricity and will sustain the force of an electric field passing through it. Also called an insulator.

Diffuse Dither is a method for printing continuous-tone images on laser printers in which the greyscale information is represented by randomly located printer dots. Diffuse dithers do not photocopy well because of the small, random, dot location in the image.

Digital is a signal represented by turning a voltage on or off. Each on or off state represents a binary 1 or 0, respectively. Unlike analogue signals, digital signals can be repeatedly regenerated without introducing noise or distortion. See also Analogue.

Digital Signature is a means of verifying the authenticity of a digital message or document, often based on asymmetric cryptography.

Digital Video is a video signal represented by computer-readable binary numbers that describe a finite set of colours and luminance levels.

Digitisation is a process of transforming analogue video signal into digital information.

DIMM stands for Dual In-line Memory Module and is a memory chip packaging that replaced the SIMM as the standard for PC memory, as unlike SIMMs, DIMMs don't have to be installed in pairs.

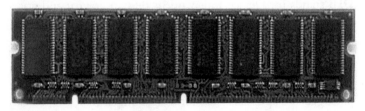

DIN Connector is a German standard used mostly for connecting keyboards, PS/2 style mice, MIDI, and Apple printer attachments.

Diode is an electronic component that acts primarily as a one-way valve.

DIP short for Dual In-Line Package and is chip housing with pins on each edge.

DIP Switch is a switch mounted on circuit board or device for configuring options.

Directory is an area or data structure in which information is stored regarding the location and contents of files and/or file structures. Also called directory partition.

DirecTV is an American direct broadcast satellite service provider owned by AT&T.

DirectX is an API used in Microsoft Windows, designed to provide software developers with direct access to low-level functions on a PC commonly used in games development.

Disk or sometimes Disc, is in general, any circular-shaped data-storage medium that stores data on the flat surface of the platter such as a magnetic disk in a hard disk drive or an optical disk in a CD, DVD or Bluray drive.

Disk Thrashing is a term that describes a hard disk drive that is constantly reading and writing data usually due to a lack of available RAM

Dithering is an image processing technique used to create the illusion of colour depth in images with a limited colour palette. For example a full-colour photograph can contain 16,777,216 colours.

Dithering is the most common method of reducing the colour range if you wanted to save the photograph as a GIF image which uses on 256 colours. The image below was converted from a full colour photograph to a 256 colour GIF.

DLL stands for Dynamic Link Library and is a packaged library containing functions that other programs can call, resources (such as icons) that other programs can use, or both. Unlike a standard programming library, whose functions are linked into an application when the application's code is compiled, an application that uses functions in a DLL links with those functions at runtime hence the term "dynamic".

DLP stands for Digital Light Processor and is an all-digital display technology that turns image data into light. Enabled by a DMD device, DLP is capable of projecting sharp, clear images of almost any size without losing any of the original image's resolution.

DMA stands for Direct Memory Access and is a process by which data moves directly between a disk drive (or other device) and main memory (RAM) without the involvement of the CPU, thus allowing the system to continue processing other tasks while the new data is being retrieved.

DMD stands for Digital Micromirror Device and is an array of semiconductor-based digital mirrors that precisely reflect a light source for projection display and hard-copy applications. A DMD enables Digital Light Processing and displays images digitally. Rather than displaying digital broadcast signals as analogue signals, a DMD directs the digital signal directly to your screen.

DMT stands for Discrete Muliti Tone and is one of the two main modulation methods that can be used with ADSL technology. DMT divides the frequency spectrum supported by standard copper twisted-pair wire into 256 sub-frequencies from 64Khz to 1.1MHz. Each sub-frequency is an independent channel and has it own stream of signals. See also CAP.

DNS stands for Domain Name System and is responsible for translating domain names into IP addresses. When you enter a URL into your browser, your computer will send the domain name to a DNS server. The DNS server responds with the IP address (eg 192.168.0.100). Your computer uses the IP address to connect to the web server.

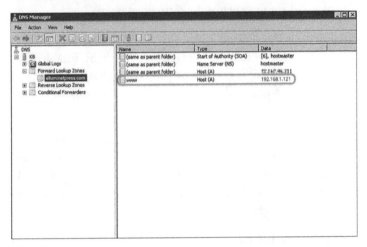

Dock In MacOS and iOS/iPadOS, the Dock is the row of app icons located across the bottom of the screen. The dock in MacOS: The dock on an iPad/iPhone:

DOCSV stands for Data Over Circuit-Switched Voice and is an ISDN adapter feature that allows data to be sent over a B-channel normally provisioned for voice, avoiding per-minute tariffs often applied to ISDN data calls.

Dolby AC-3 is a perceptual digital audio coding technique capable of delivering multichannel digital surround sound. It incorporates 6 (5.1) discrete channels; each channel can carry a different signal simultaneously (left front, right front, centre, left rear, right rear, sub- woofer).

Dolby Digital is a digital audio encoding system from Dolby used in movie and home theatres that employs Dolby's AC-3 coding and compression technology to provide six channels of audio, known as 5.1 for front left, front right, front center, rear left, rear right and subwoofer.

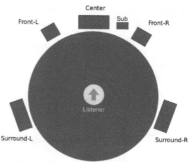

Domain is usually used to describe a group of users or computers on a network.

Domain Name identifies a network domain, a resource, or a server hosting a website. The top-level domains such as .com, .co.uk, .edu, .gov, and .org are the highest level of domain names. Second-level domains commonly refer to the organization. Each organization can also have sub-domains for different services such as website (www), mail servers (mail), or an e-commerce site (shop).

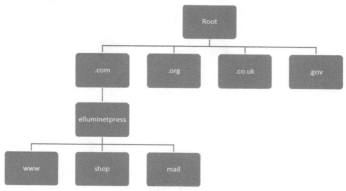

Doping is the introduction of an element that alters the conductivity of a semiconductor. Adding boron to silicon will create a P-type(more positive) material, while adding phosphorus or arsenic to silicon will create N-type (more negative) material.

Dot Matrix is a type of printer that uses one or two columns of dot hammers behind an ink ribbon to form text and images out of dots. The more dot hammers used, the higher the resolution of the printed image.

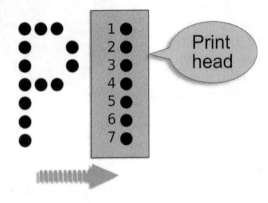

Dot Pitch is the distance between the centres of two same-colour phosphor dots on the screen. The closer the dots, the smaller the dot pitch, and the sharper the image. See also Stripe Pitch.

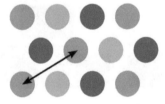

Dot Trio is the standard triad arrangement of the three primary colours on a screen.

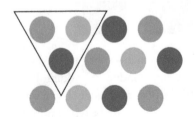

DPMS stands for Display Power Management Signalling and is a monitor that comply with this can be managed by Power Management features found in CMOS configuration on Energy Saving PCs.

DQM Data Mask is the control signal used by SDRAMs to provide byte masking during read and write operations. There is one DQM signal for every 8 bits of data width.

DRAM stands for Dynamic Random Access Memory and is the memory used to store data in personal computers. DRAM stores each bit of information in a cell composed of a capacitor and a transistor. Because the capacitor in a DRAM cell can hold a charge for only a few milliseconds, DRAM must be continually refreshed in order to retain its data. See also EDO RAM and SRAM.

DRDRAM stands for Direct Rambus DRAM and is a RAM architecture developed by Rambus in the 1990s through to the early-2000s.

Drive Bay is a 5.25in or 3.5in wide bay used to house disk drives in a computer's case such as a hard disk or DVD-ROM. Bays can be hidden for internal drives such as a hard disk or exposed for a DVD-ROM drive.

Drive Geometry is the number of heads, cylinders, and sectors per track of a disk drive.

Driver is a program used by an operating system to control a device such as a graphics card, printer, scanner, or other peripheral device. Most hardware manufacturers produce drivers for their devices.

DSP stands for Digital Signal Processor and is an electronic device designed to convert an analogue signal into a digital data stream (and vice-versa). DSPs are used in a variety of devices such as personal computers, high speed modems, sound cards, and real-time audio/video compression and decompression hardware.

DSP Solution is the use of a Digital Signal Processor in conjunction with mixed-signal devices and embedded software to collect, process, compress, transmit and display the analogue and digital data found in today's most popular multimedia applications.

DSS stands for Digital Satellite System, a network of satellites that broadcast digital data. An example of a DSS is DirecTV, which broadcasts digital television signals.

DSSS stands for Direct-Sequence Spread Spectrum and is one of two types of spread spectrum radio that continuously changes frequencies or signal patterns. DSSS multiplies the data bits by a very fast pseudo-random bit pattern that "spreads" the data into a large coded stream that takes the full bandwidth of the channel.

D-SUB Connector is a common "D" shaped electrical connector used to connect computer peripherals together such as monitors or serial devices. A common D-Sub connector was used to connect a monitor to a PC. Below: serial and VGA

DTCP stands for Digital Transmission Content Protection and is a system devised for secure transmission in the home environment over two-way transmission lines such as the FireWire bus. DTCP prevents unauthorised copying of digital content while allowing legitimate copying for purposes such as time shifting.

DTE stands for Data Terminal Equipment and is an end device on a communications circuit such as a PC or workstation.

DTR stands for Data Transfer Rate and is the speed at which data is transferred between a host and a data recording device. Usually noted in KBps or MBps, and sometimes in MB/minute. Can mean a "peak" rather than a "sustained" transfer rate.

Dual Boot allows a computer to house and boot two different operating systems such as Windows and Linux.

Duplex is a point to point communication system that allows two or more devices to communicate. Half duplex transmissions, only one device can send data at a time. Full duplex transmissions allow both devices communicate simultaneously.

DV is a consumer digital video format that uses 1/4" (6.35mm) metal evaporated tape, recorded at 25 Mbps on MiniDV cassettes providing up to 90 minutes of record time in long-play mode.

DVB stands for Digital Video Broadcasting project and is a European consortia that developed a set of standards that define digital broadcasting using existing satellite, cable, and terrestrial transmission. See also ATSC.

DVD stands for Digital Video Disc or Digital Versatile Disc is an optical storage medium used to store digital data such as computer files, software, videos and films. There are a few different types of DVD disc: Single sided discs can hold 4.7 GB of data. Roughly 2 hours of video at standard definition.

Single sided Dual layer discs can hold 8.5 GB of data - roughly 4 hours of video at standard definition. Double sided single layer discs can hold 9.4 GB of data. Double sided dual layer discs can hold 17.08 GB of data. The surface of the disc is marked with pits. This is how the data is encoded onto the disc. Each time a pit is encountered, the laser beam is not reflected and is interpreted as a 0. If there is no pit, the laser beam is reflected and is interpreted as a 1.

Here we can see the inside of a DVD drive

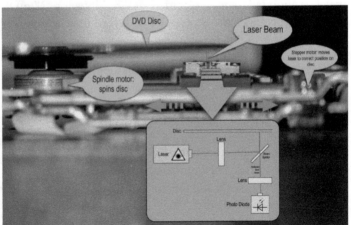

Here is a view from the top of the drive

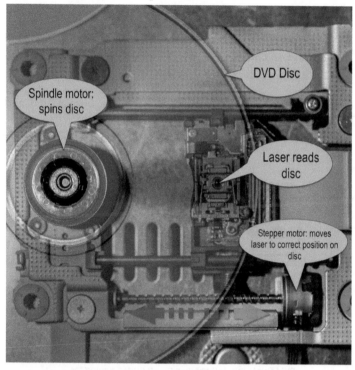

DVD-Audio is the DVD audio-only storage format similar to CD- Audio. DVD-Audio is facing stiff competition from a number of other high fidelity audio standards.

DVI is a digital interface for connecting to computer monitors and projectors. There are three types DVI-I, DVI-D and DVI-A.

DVI-A short for DVI-Analog and is an analog only format that supports resolutions of up to 1920x1200.

DVI-D short for DVI-Digital only carries digital signals and can be dual or single link. DVI-D supports resolutions of up to 1920x1200 single link, or 2560x1600 dual link.

DVI-I short for DVI-Integrated supports both digital and analog signals and can be dual or single link. DVI-I supports resolutions of up to 1920x1200 single link, or 2560x1600 dual link.

DVI-I Single Link. DVI cable with integrated analog for both analog and digital displays up to 1920 × 1200

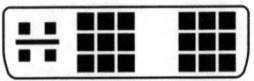

DVI-I Dual Link. DVI cable with integrated analog for both analog and digital displays up to 2560 × 1600

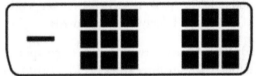

DVI-D Digital Single Link. DVI cable with digital signal only for displays up to 1920 × 1200

DVI-D Digital Dual Link. DVI cable with digital signal only for displays up to 2560 × 1900

Dye-Sublimation is a specialist print technology used for demanding graphic arts and photographic applications that require continuous tone output.

Dynamic Disk is a feature in Windows operating systems that allow a user to resize a volume or to span it across multiple drives. Dynamic disks can be also be striped or mirrored to provide performance gains and fault tolerance.

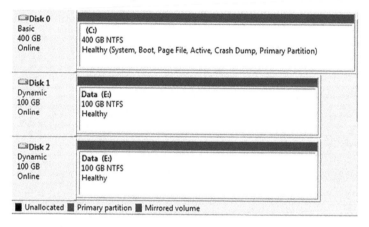

Dynamic Power Management Architecture is Intel's extensive set of power management features with emphasis on power conservation.

E

E1 is a four-wire European telephone company standard that carries data at 2.048 Mbit/s, equivalent of a US T1 line.

EAX stands for Environmental Audio Extensions and is a now deprecated hardware and software audio standard developed by Creative Labs, used originally in the SoundBlaster cards.

ECC stands for Error Correction Code and is a system used to detect errors that can be corrected by the device's controller when the data is read. See also CRC.

ECMA stands for European Computer Manufacturers Association and is a non-profit international industry association founded in 1961 dedicated to the worldwide standardisation of information and communication systems.

EDAP stands for Extended Data Availability and Protection and was Created by the RAID Advisory Board in 1997.

EDGE stands for Enhanced Data for GSM Evolution and is a mobile phone technology that was developed as an extension to GSM that allows improved data rates.

EDO DRAM stands for Extended Data Out Random Access Memory and is a form of DRAM that has a two-stage pipeline, allowing the memory controller to read data while it is being reset for the next operation.

EDP stands for Enhanced Dot Pitch and is Hitachi's tube technology in which the phosphor triads are spaced closer together horizontally than they are vertically.

EDRAM stands for Enhanced Dynamic Random Access Memory and is a form of DRAM that boosts performance by placing a small complement of static RAM (SRAM) in each DRAM chip and using the SRAM as a cache. Also known as cached DRAM, or CDRAM.

EDVAC stands for Electronic Discrete Variable Automatic Computer and was the first computer to incorporate Von Neumann's stored program concept, in which the programme executed by the computer was stored as data, rather than existing as wire connections. Designed in 1946, when EDVAC became fully operational in 1952 it contained approximately 4,000 vacuum tubes and 10,000 crystal diodes.

EEPROM stands for Electrically Erasable Programmable Read Only Memory: a special type of read-only memory (ROM) that can be erased and written electrically. EEPROM maintains its contents without power backup and is frequently used for system-board BIOS's.

EGA is IBM's standard for colour displays prior to the VGA standard. It specified a resolution of 640×350 with up to 256 colours and a 9-pin (DB-9) connector.

EIA stands for Electronic Industries Association: a trade association representing the U.S. high technology community which began life in 1924 as the Radio Manufacturers Association. It has been responsible for developing some important standards, such as the RS-232, RS-422 and RS-423 standards for connecting serial devices. In 1988, it spun off its Information & Telecommunications Technology Group into a separate organisation known as the TIA.

EIDE stands for Enhanced Integrated Device Electronics or

Enhanced Intelligent Drive Electronics: an enhanced version of the IDE drive interface that expands the maximum disk size from 504Mb to 8.4Gb, more than doubles the maximum data transfer rate, and supports up to four drives per PC (as opposed to two in IDE systems). EIDE's primary competitor is SCSI-2, which also supports large hard disks and high transfer rates.

EISA stands for Extended Industry Standard Architecture: an open 32-bit extension to the ISA 16-bit bus standard designed by Compaq, AST and other clone makers in response to IBM's proprietary MCA (Micro Channel Architecture) 32-bit bus design. Unlike the Micro Channel, an EISA bus is backward-compatible with 8-bit and 16-bit expansion cards designed for the ISA bus.

EIST stands for Enhanced Intel Speed Step technology: an enhanced version of Intel's Speed Step technology which dynamically scales the speed of a processor between its default clock setting and a minimum speed, based on how much CPU horsepower is needed at that moment, so as to both reduce power consumption and heat.

EM64T is short for Extended Memory 64 Technology: an enhancement to Intel's IA-32 architecture which allows a processor to run newly written 64-bit code and access larger amounts of memory when used with a 64-bit OS and application. These extensions do not run code written for the Intel Itanium processor.

Embedded Servo is the device some disk drives use to move the head a tracks.

Embedded System is a computer control system that is built into a device such as the control system in a car, washing machine or a microwave oven.

Encoding is the process of converting data into another form.

Digital video from a camera can be encoded using H264 or MPEG, an image from a camera can be encoded using JPEG. Characters on a keyboard can be encoded in binary using ASCII.

Encryption is a method used to convert data into an unrecognisable form using a cryptographic key.

Energy Star launched in 1993, this is a program established by the Environmental Protection Agency (EPA) as a partnership with the computer industry to promote the introduction of energy-efficient personal computers which help reduce air pollution caused by power generation. To comply with the Energy Star guidelines, a computer system or monitor must consume less than 30 watts of power in its lowest power state.

EPP stands for Enhanced Parallel Port: a parallel port that conforms to the EPP standard developed by the IEEE 1284 standards committee. The EPP specification transforms a parallel port into an expansion bus that can handle up to 64 disk drives, tape drives, CD-ROM drives, and other mass-storage devices.

EPROM is short for Erasable Programmable Read Only Memory and is a memory chip that can store programs and data in a non-volatile state, meaning the chip retains the memory when the power is cut. These devices are erased by high-intensity ultraviolet (UV) light and can then reprogrammed.

Error is an unexpected result due to a bug or flaw in a program or a hardware fault

Error Control is the encoding of text or data so that a receiver can detect and correct errors in data transmissions.

Error Message is a message displayed to the user when a problem or fault occurs.

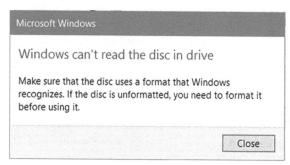

Microsoft Windows

Windows can't read the disc in drive

Make sure that the disc uses a format that Windows recognizes. If the disc is unformatted, you need to format it before using it.

Close

eSATA cables connect to some types of high speed external portable hard drives. The eSATA cable cannot transmit power, unless you use eSATAp (powered eSATA).

Escape Sequence is a sequence of three characters (normally "+++") that switches the modem from the on-line mode to the command mode without breaking the telephone connection.

ESCD is a region of non-volatile memory used by BIOS and ICU (Intel Configuration Utility) or PnP operating system to record information about the current configuration of the system.

ESDI stands for Enhanced Small Device Interface: an interface standard developed by a consortium of the leading PC manufacturers for connecting disk drives to PCs. Introduced in the early 1980s, ESDI was two to three times faster than the older ST-506 standard. It has long since been superseded by the IDE, EIDE and SCSI interfaces.

Etch is a process using a chemical bath (wet etch) or a plasma (dry etch) that removes unwanted substances from the wafer surface.

Ethernet is a networking technology used to connect computers and devices together and is commonly used in LANs. Ethernet can transfer data at 100Mbps on some cables and 1Gbps – 10Gbps on high speed cables.

Ethernet Switch is a multiport layer 2 hardware device that connects devices such as PCs, Wireless APs, servers, or printers to a computer network.

ETSI stands for European Telecommunications Standards Institute: a non- profit membership organisation founded in 1988, dedicated to standardising telecommunications throughout Europe. It promotes worldwide standards, and its efforts are co-ordinated with the ITU.

Execute is to carry out an instruction.

exFAT is short for Extensible File Allocation Table and is a file system optimized for USB flash drives, external hard drives, and memory cards. exFAT has a maximum volume size of 128PB, and a maximum file size of 16 EB. This is a useful file format for formatting external drives as it provides compatibility across different operating systems such as Windows and MacOS.

Expansion Bus is an input/output bus typically comprised of a series of slots on the motherboard. Expansion boards are plugged into the bus. ISA, EISA, PCI express and VL-Bus are examples of expansion buses used in a PC.

Expansion Card is a circuit board that fits into a computer expansion slot to add a certain function (like a modem, sound card, or SCSI interface).

Expert System is an artificial intelligence system designed to emulate decision making using an inference engine attached to a knowledge database.

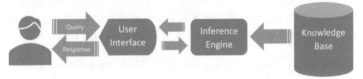

Expert systems are often used in healthcare and customer service.

External Hard Drive is an external hard drive is a permanent storage device that sits outside a computer and is usually connected using a USB cable.

Extrusion Taking a flat, 2-D object and adding a z plane to expand it into 3-D space.

F

FAQ stands for Frequently Asked Questions and as its name suggests is a list of questions and answers that are most commonly asked by customers or users of a system or product.

FAT stands for File Allocation Table and is the file system used by MS-DOS and Windows to manage and store files on a hard disks, external hard disk, memory card of flash drive. The file system takes its name from an on-disk data structure known as the file allocation table, which records where individual portions of each file are located on the disk.

FAT16 is a file system used in early versions of Windows. FAT16 had a maximum volume size of 4GB, and a maximum file size of 2GB.

FAT32 is a file system used in Windows 98, which supports larger partition sizes and smaller cluster sizes than FAT16, thereby improving disk performance and increasing available disk space. FAT32 has a maximum volume size of 8TB - however Windows only formats FAT32 volumes up to 32GB. You can have a maximum file size of 4GB.

FCC stands for Federal Communications Commission and is the U.S. Government agency that supervises, licenses, and regulates electronic and electromagnetic transmission standards.

FCPGA stands for Flip Chip Plastic Grid Array and is a micro CPU package, for socketable boards, consisting of a die placed face-down on an organic substrate. The package uses 478 pins, which are 2.03 mm long and .32 mm in diameter.

FDD is an interface which allows a floppy drive to be connected to the motherboard.

FDDI stands for Fibre Distributed Data Interface and is an ANSI standard token ring network that uses optical fibre cabling and transmits at 100 Mbit/s up to two kilometres. Typically used as backbones for wide area networks (WANs).

FDMA stands for Frequency Division Multiple Access and is a mobile communications technique in which the radio spectrum is divided into frequency bands.

Feathering is a term used when describing printed text quality. Feathering occurs when deposited ink follows the contours of the paper. Depending on the viscosity of the ink, the rougher the grain of the paper the more pronounced the feathering will be.

FED stands for Field Emission Display: a display technology which use vacuum tubes (one for each pixel) with conventional RGB phosphors.

Fetch Execute Cycle is the basic operating cycle used by the CPU to retrieve or fetch and instruction from memory, then decode and execute it.

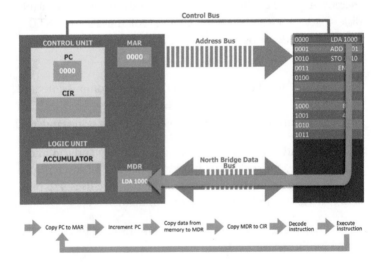

FHSS stands for Frequency Hopping Spread Spectrum and is radio transmission method that continuously changes the Centre frequency of a carrier several times per second according to a pseudo-random set of channels, thereby making illegal monitoring extremely difficult, if not impossible. See also DSSS.

Fiber is a long distance medium for telecommunications and computer data networking where data is transmitted by sending pulses of infrared light through the optical fiber.

Fiber-optic Communication is a method of transmitting data by sending pulses of infrared light through a fiber optic cable.

Field is a data unit found on a table in a database used to store a value such as a name. Also an element on a user interface designed to accept data from a user such as a search field on a web page.

FIFO stands for First In-First Out and is a storage method that retrieves the item stored for the longest time (ie the first item in). See also LIFO.

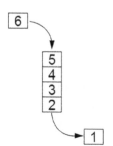

File is an object that contains data. A file can be a Word document, a photograph, a video, or music.

File Explorer formerly known as Windows Explorer, is an app used for browsing and managing files in Windows 10. You'll find the icon on your taskbar.

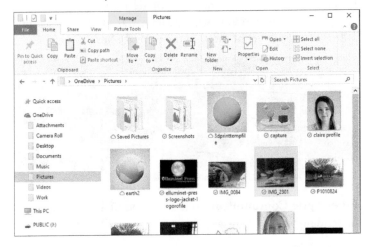

File Server is a computer on a network that provides devices access to centralised shared files.

File System specifies how data is organised and stored on a storage medium such as a hard disk drive. File systems are usually hierarchical meaning the data is organised allowing the user to organise their files into directories or folders. Common examples are: NTFS on Windows, HFS or APFS on a Mac, or EXT on linux

File Transfer Protocol is a protocol used for transferring files to and from a remote machine usually over port 21. FTP either runs in active or passive mode. In active mode, the client opens a port on the local machine. Once the client issues a command to transfer a file, the server connects to the port on the client. In passive mode the client initiates both sides of the connection. When the client issues a command to transfer a file, the client establishes a connection to the server. Passive mode is the most common.

Fill Factor is used in connection with digital display technologies (such as LCD and DLP) to convey how much of the area of a single pixel is used for the image as opposed to the grid surrounding the pixel. The higher the "fill factor" the better. See also Screen Door Effect.

Filtering is a process used in both analogue and digital image processing to reduce bandwidth. Filters can be designed to remove information content such as high or low frequencies, for example, or to average adjacent pixels, creating a new value from two or more pixels.

Finder is a file management app used on the Apple Macintosh computers. You'll find the finder app located on the bottom left of the dock.

Firewall is a hardware device or computer program that resides between an internal network or computer and the Internet. It can be configured to allow only specific kinds of messages from the Internet to pass to the internal network, thereby protecting it from intruders or hackers who might try to use the Internet to break into those systems.

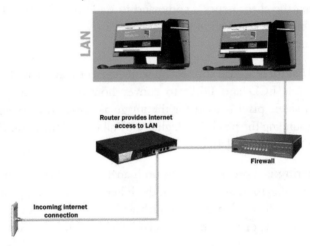

FireWire also known as IEEE 1394 or iLink. An international high- performance serial-bus standard that offers the real-time data transfer of video, audio and peripheral applications through a universal I/O interface. With this technology, digital cameras, CD-ROMs, printers, hard-disk drives and audio/stereo equipment can move data at high speeds to desktops and portable computers through a single cable.

Firmware is a program loaded directly into a ROM or EEPROM chip for controlling the operation of the computer or peripheral devices. Distinct from software, which is stored in read/write memory and can be altered.

Fixed Point Number is a number that has a fixed number of digits after the decimal point.

Flash Drive is a data storage device that uses flash memory to store data and can be plugged into a USB port.

Flash Memory is a non-volatile memory device that retains its data when the power is removed. The device is similar to EPROM with the exception that it can be electrically erased, whereas an EPROM must be exposed to ultra-violet light to erase. Commonly used in digital cameras.

Flash ROM is a type of memory used for firmware in modems and other digital devices. Unlike conventional ROM (read-only memory), flash ROM can be erased and reprogrammed, making it possible to update a product's firmware without re-placing memory chips.

Flat Panel Display is a thin display screen that uses any of a number of technologies, such as LCD, plasma and FED. Traditionally used in laptops, flat panel displays are slowly beginning to replace desktop CRTs for specialised applications.

Flat Shading is the simplest form of 3D shading which fills polygons with one colour. Processor overheads are negligible and 3D games will allow the graphics to be stripped down to flat shading to improve the frame rate.

Floating Point numbers are those that contain floating decimal points such as 88.87, 955.35, 0.06. For example, the number 454.75 can be expressed as

$$4.5475 * 10^2$$

4.5475 is called the mantissa. The 2 is the exponent (this tells you where to move the decimal point), and 10 is the number base (in this case decimal base 10). Similarly 0.0025 can be expressed as

$$2.5 * 10^{-3}$$

Floppy Drive is somewhat obsolete nowadays and was included in most PCs. The 3.5in high density floppy disk could hold 1.44MB of data. Older floppy disks were 5.25in disks.

Flow Control is the mechanism that regulates the flow of data between two devices. Modems typically have two methods of flow control software flow control (XON/XOFF) and hardware flow control (CTS/RTS).

Flux Density is the number of magnetic field patterns that can be stored on a given area of disk surface, used as a measure of data density. The number is usually stated as flux changes per inch (FCI), with typical values in the tens of thousands.

Fly Height is the distance between the read/write head and the disk surface. A cushion of air keeps the head from hitting the surface of the disk. Smaller fly heights allow denser data storage but require more precise mechanics.

FM is short for Frequency Modulation and is a data transmission technique that encodes the data by varying (or modulating) the frequency of the carrier wave.

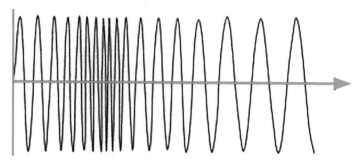

FM Synthesis is short for Frequency Modulation Synthesis and is an outdated technique for synthesising music reproduction but still widely supported to provide compatibility with older games software.

Font is a typeface of a certain point size, weight and style. For example: Times New Roman is a typeface. **Times New Roman Bold**, Times New Roman Regular, or *Times New Roman Italic* are all fonts.

For Loop is a flow control statement is a programming language used to execute a section of code repeatedly for a set number of times. For example, reading items in a list using Python.

```
cars = ["merc", "bmw", "audi"]
for x in cars:
    print(x)
```

Form Factor is the size, shape, and physical arrangement of computer components such as motherboards, add on cards, power supplies, disk drives and so on. The physical size of a device as measured by outside dimensions. With regard to a disk drive, the form factor is the overall diameter of the platters and case, such as 3.5in or 5.25in, not the size in terms of storage capacity. If the drive is a 5.25in form factor it means that the drive is the same size as a 5.25in diskette drive and uses the same fixing points.

Format is a process of preparing a storage medium such as a hard disk drive for an operating system to store data using a file system such as NTFS, FAT32 or exFAT.

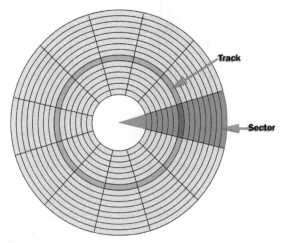

Also the way in which something is arranged or set out such as a document format

Formatted Capacity is the amount of space left to store data on a disk after writing the sector headers, boundary definitions, and timing information during a format operation. The size of a drive always is reported in formatted capacity, accurately reflecting the usable space available.

FPM DRAM stands for Fast Page Mode RAM and is a timing option that permits several bits of data in a single row on a DRAM chip to be accessed at an accelerated rate. Fast Page Mode involves selecting multiple column addresses in rapid succession once the row address has been selected.

FPS stands for Frames Per Second and is the number of frames shown in each second of time.

FPU is short for Floating Point Unit and is a part of the computer's CPU that performs floating point calculations. See Floating Point.

Fractals are never-ending repeating patterns such as the Mandelbrot Set

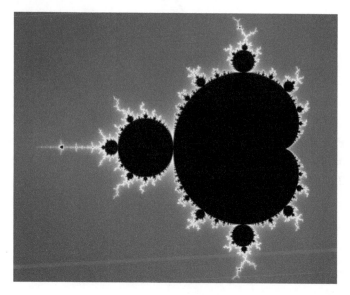

Frame is a single, complete picture in a video. Also a unit of data transmission on a computer network.

Frame Buffer is a buffer often used in display memory that temporarily stores a full frame of picture at one time.

Frame Grabber is a device that captures a frame from a full motion video.

Frame Rate is how many frames a screen displays in one second. NTSC shows 30 frames per second. PAL is 25 frames per second.

Front Projection is when a projector is positioned in front of the screen. See also Rear Projection.

Front Side Bus is the data bus that connects the CPU to the main memory (RAM).

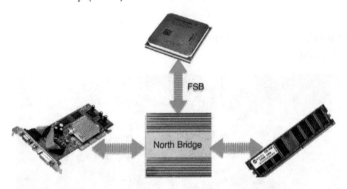

FSK stands for Frequency Shift Keying and is a data transmission technique that encodes data into a carrier wave by varying the frequency.

FST is short for Flat Square Tube and describes the viewing surface of a cathode ray tube that is nearly flat. Flatter screens give the appearance of straighter lines, and they can aid in the reduction of glare, compared to conventional tubes.

FTP stands for File Transfer Protocol and is a protocol for transferring files to and from a remote machine usually over port 21. FTP either runs in active or passive mode. In active mode, the client opens a port on the local machine. Once the client issues a command to transfer a file, the server connects to the port on the client. In passive mode the client initiates both sides of the connection. When the client issues a command to transfer a file, the client establishes a connection to the server. Passive mode is the most common.

FTTC stands for Fibre to the Cabinet. The fibre optic cable runs from the exchange to the telephone cabinet in your street and uses vDSL over the copper phone line to run the last 100-300m or so to your house.

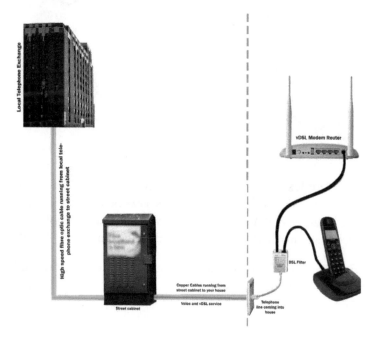

FTTP stands for Fibre to the Premises. The fibre optic cable runs from the telephone exchange to the socket on the wall in your house. The fibre optic cable will plug into a modem supplied by your ISP which will connect you to the internet.

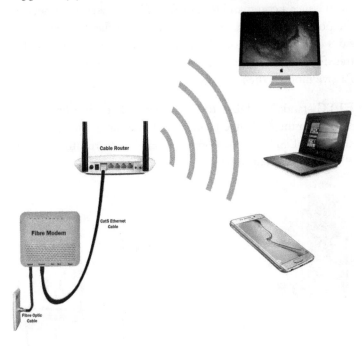

Full-Duplex is often used in reference to communications channels or devices and means that data can be sent and received at the same time. Also used to describe a soundcard's ability to record and playback digital audio at the same time.

Full-Motion Video is video shown at 30 frames per second (NTSC), 25 frames per second.

G

Gain is the increase in signalling power as an audio signal is boosted by an electronic device. It is measured in decibels.

Gamma is a mathematical curve representing both the contrast and brightness of an image. Moving the curve in one direction will make the image both darker and decrease the contrast. Moving the curve the other direction will make the image both lighter and decrease the contrast.

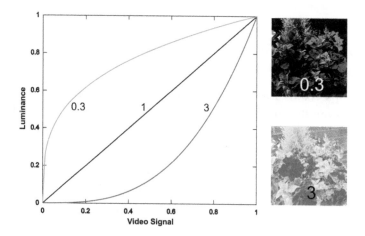

Gamma Correction is used to correct the differences between the way a camera captures an image and the way a monitor displays the image in order to display the image accurately.

Gamut is the range of colours that can be captured or represented by a device.

Gateway is a hardware device that serves as a bridge between two different types of network and that contains the necessary protocol translation software to enable them to exchange information. The router that your ISP sends you acts as a gateway between your home network and the internet.

GB stands for Gigabyte, a unit of data storage equivalent to 1 billion bytes (1,073,741,824 bytes).

GBps stands for GigaBytes per second, a data rate used to measure the speed of a network or, mass storage devices and memory systems.

GDI short for Graphical Device Interface, a component of Windows that allows applications to draw on screens, printers, and other output devices. A GDI compliant printer will print exactly what is displayed on a Windows screen without having to transpose it into a printer.

General MIDI is a table of 128 standard sounds or instruments for MIDI cards and synthesisers.

Gflops is short for Gigaflops equalling 1 thousand million floating-point instructions per second.

Ghosting a colloquial term describing the practice of ending all communication with someone. Also on a computer monitor an effect found in fast moving scenes where objects leave a trail of pixels.

GiB stands for Gibibyte and is a unit of measure consisting of 1024MiB.

GIF is short for Graphics Interchange Format and is an image limited to 256 colours with transparency commonly found on the web.

Gigabit Ethernet is a version of Ethernet that runs at 1Gbps.

GOP is a group of frames between successive I frames, the others being P and/or B frames of an MPEG movie. The GOP concept allows the temporal redundancy across frames (from frame to frame) for video content to be reduced.

GOPS stands for Giga Operations Per Second: in the case of multimedia processing, more GOPS translate to better video quality.

Gouraud Shading is a method of hiding the boundaries between polygons by modulating the light intensity across each one in a polygon mesh.

GPF short for General Protection Fault and is an error triggered when a Windows program tries to access memory used by another process.

GPRS stands for General Packet Radio Service and is an enhancement for GSM and TDMA core networks that introduces packet data transmission. GPRS uses radio spectrum very efficiently and provides users with "always on" connectivity and greater bandwidth.

GPS stands for Global Positioning System and is a satellite-based positioning system that provides a three-dimensional position on the Earth's surface, commonly used navigation systems such as satellite navigation (sat-nav).

GPT stands for GUID Partition Table and is the scheme used to define hard disk partitions on computers with UEFI firmware. GPT replaces MBR.

GPU stands for Graphics Processing Unit and is responsible for processing video, graphic and visual effects you see on your monitor.

Gradient in graphics, is a area with a smooth blend from one colour to another.

Graphic User Interface or Graphical User Interface (GUI), is a system of interactive visual components such as windows, menus and icons used to convey information to the user and represent commands and applications. The user clicks on icons to start apps, and selects commands from menus to execute operations or tasks.

Information is conveyed to the user using dialog boxes or windows. Microsoft Windows, MacOS, iOS, Linux, and Android all use a Graphic User Interfaces.

Graphics Card or video card is responsible for processing video, graphics and visual effects you see on your monitor. The graphics card is also known as a GPU (graphics processing unit).

Graphics Library is a programming library that includes a defined set of primitives and function calls that enable the programmer to draw lines and create shapes in a computer program.

Graphics Processor is the specialised processor at the heart of the graphics card. Modern chipsets can also integrate video processing, 3D polygon setup and texturing routines, and, in some cases, the RAMDAC.

Greyscale is shades of grey that represent light and dark portions of an image. Colour images can also be converted to greyscale where the colours are represented by various shades of grey.

GSM stands for Global System for Mobile Communications and was first introduced in 1991. GSM was implemented using the 400MHz, 900MHz, 1800MHz and 1900MHz frequency bands.

GUI see Graphic User Interface

GUID stands for Globally Unique Identifier and is a 128bit identifier used to uniquely identify user accounts in windows, as well as documents, hardware components, and applications.

Guide Rails are the plastic or metal strips attached to the sides of a hard disk drive mounted in an IBM compatible computer so that the drive easily slides into place.

H.264 also known as Advanced Video Coding (AVC) or MPEG-4 part 10 and is a popular video codec for encoding high quality video used in digital broadcast, internet, and video streaming services.

H.265 also known as High Efficiency Video Coding (HEVC) and is the successor to H.264. H.265 offers more efficient compression and enables encoding and streaming of HD, 4K and 8K video.

Half Adder is a combination logic circuit used in the addition of two bits.

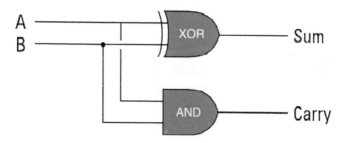

A half adder consists of an eXclusive OR and an AND gate.

A	B	Sum	Carry
0	0	0	0
0	1	1	0
1	0	1	0
1	1	0	1

Half-Duplex is data transmission in both directions, but only in one direction at a time.

Halftone is a method of expressing colour gradation in continuous tone images. The image is resolved into dots, with dark colour being expressed by a large number of dots and diluted colour is by a smaller number of dots. The dot patterns used are called dithers.

Handoff is a continuity feature available on apple devices that allows you to start a task on one device and finish it on another.

Handshake is an automated process of negotiation between two devices preceding a connection.

Hard Disk is a storage medium that stores data as magnetic patterns on a rigid disk, usually made of a magnetic thin film deposited on an aluminium or glass platter. Magnetic read/write heads are mounted on an actuator arm that moves back and forth across the surface of the platter.

Hard Error is a data error that occurs on a disk and is usually caused by defects in the surface.

Harvard Architecture developed in early computer systems where instructions and data were stored on punch cards or punched paper tape. The photograph below is the Harvard Mark I built by IBM in 1944.

The Mark I read its instructions from a punched paper tape. A separate tape contained data for input. This separation of data and instructions is known as the Harvard architecture.

Here in the diagram below, you can see on the Harvard architecture, there is a separate area for program instructions and another for data.

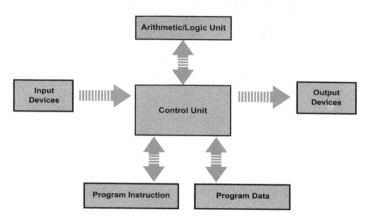

Many embedded systems in use today are based on the Harvard architecture.

HDCP stands for High-bandwidth Digital Content Protection and is an old encoding method used for distributing digital content via a DP, DVI or HDMI. Using hardware on both the graphics card and the monitor, HDCP encrypts data on route to a display device, where it is then decrypted.

HDLC stands for High-level Data Link Control and is an ISO communications protocol used in X.25 packet switching networks. The HDLC protocol embeds information in a data frame that allows devices to control data flow and correct errors at the data link layer.

HDMI stands for High Definition Media Interface and is an interface for connecting to TVs, monitors, projectors, set top boxes, dvd/bluray players, media streaming devices and so forth. This interface carries both digital audio and video on a single cable. There are three sizes of connectors: standard, mini and micro.

Standard   Mini   Micro

HDTV short for High Definition TV and is a television system with a resolution greater than 525- line and 625-line systems and a picture aspect ratio of 16:9. Common HDTV formats:

720p (1280x720) with 921,600 pixels.

1080i (1920×1080) interlaced scan with 1,036,800 pixels.

1080p (1920×1080) progressive scan with 2,073,600 pixels:

Head is the tiny electromagnetic coil used to read and write magnetic data patterns on a disk.

Head Crash is damage to a read / write head on a magnetic disk, caused when the head hit the disk surface. A head crash can also be caused by dust and other contamination inside the drive enclosure.

Heat Sink is a metallic structure attached to a semiconductor device such as a CPU, that dissipates the heat to the surrounding environment.

HEVC or H.265, is short for High Efficiency Video Coding and is a video compression standard that offers better compression to H.264. See H.265.

Hexadecimal also known as base 16, and is a numbering system of 16 digits often used as a short hand for binary notation. Hexadecimal uses the numbers 0-9, and the letters A-F:

Hex	0	1	2	3	4	5	6	7	8	9	A	B	C	D	E	F
Dec	0	1	2	3	4	5	6	7	8	9	10	11	12	13	14	15

131

Hierarchical Database is a database where the data is organized into a tree-like structure with a single parent for each record

High Colour is any graphics that are 16-bit and contain up to 65,536 colours.

High-Level Formatting is disk format operation performed by the operating system's format program such as the format command in Linux or Windows 10. Among other things, the formatting program creates the root directory, file allocation tables, and other basic configurations. See also Low-Level Formatting.

High-Level Language is a computer programming language that allows a programmer to write programs in a more human-like language that focuses on logic rather than a particular type of computer hardware. Code is then either compiled or interpreted for execution. Examples include C, C++, Python, and Java

Highlights are the bright parts of an image (eg the sky).

Histogram is a graphical representation of the tonal distribution in a digital image. The sky is represented by the highlights and whites as these are the brightest tones. In contrast the darkest parts of the image are represented by the blacks and shadows.

Home Theatre system is a audio visual system combining components such as live TV, DVD and video streaming at home in order to recreate the experience of watching a movie in the cinema.

Host is any device connected to a TCP/IP network such as the internet, that has a live IP address.

Host Adapter is a circuit board or card that plugs into a slot on the motherboard and acts as the interface between the system bus and a peripheral device.

Hot Swap is the removal or addition of components to a computer system without first shutting down. With a hot swapping, you can add a hard disk or remove it while the computer system is running.

Hostname is a unique name for a device on a network that is used to identify the device in electronic communication.

HPM short for Hyper Page Mode, in DRAM operation, another term for EDO or Extended Data Out.

HRTF stands for Head-Related Transfer Functions and refers to the mathematics that models the way a human ear localises the direction of a sound.

HSB short for Hue Saturation Brightness, a way of describing colour in a more human friendly way. With the HSB model, all colours can be defined by expressing their levels of hue as a number of degrees on the colour wheel.

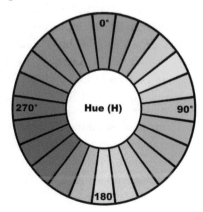

Saturation and brightness are expressed as a percentage. The saturation is the intensity of the hue.

Here in Photoshop's colour picker we can see the HSB values for the selected colour.

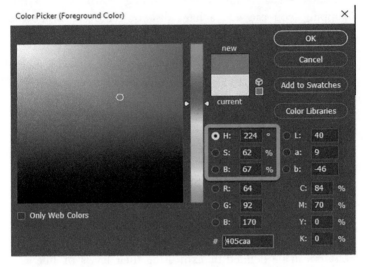

HSCSD stands for High Speed Circuit Switched Data and is the final evolution of circuit switched data within the GSM environment. HSCSD enables the transmission of data over a GSM link at speeds of up to 57.6kbit/s. This is achieved by concatenating consecutive GSM timeslots, each of which is capable of supporting 14.4kbit/s. Up to four GSM timeslots are needed for the transmission of HSCSD.

HSF stands for Horizontal Scanning Frequency and indicates the speed, measured in kilohertz, at which a single horizontal line is drawn on the screen. Higher scan rates are needed to provide sharper, crisper images at higher resolutions. Also called scan rate.

HTML stands for Hypertext Markup Language and is an ASCII text-based, script- like language used for creating hypertext documents for the World Wide Web.

HTPS stands for High Temperature Poly-Silicon and is a thin-film transistor (TFT) panel is an active matrix display containing a microscopic thin-film transistor in the corner of each pixel. HTPS panels allow driver ICs to be embedded into their TFTs, thereby allowing greater miniaturisation (higher pixel counts and higher aperture ratios).

HTTP stands for Hypertext Transfer Protocol and is the way a web browser and the server communicate to deliver web pages. http://www.elluminetpress.com

HTTPS stands for Hypertext Transfer Protocol Secure and is the way a web browser server communicate to deliver web pages. The protocol builds on HTTP by adding a secure encrypted connection between server and host using Transport Layer Security (TLS) or Secure Sockets Layer (SSL). https://www.elluminetpress.com

Hub

Hub is more or less obsolete nowadays. A hub was a common connection point for devices in a network, often used at the centre of a star-topology network. A hub is a multiport repeater, a packet entering a port on the hub is broadcast to every other port. Network switches have largely replaced hubs on ethernet networks.

Hue is another word for colour often used as a term for the pure spectrum colours such as red, orange, yellow, blue, green, and violet.

Huffman Coding is a lossless data compression algorithm based on the frequency of occurrence of a data item. Codes of different lengths are assigned to characters based on the frequency of occurrence. Smaller codes are assigned to characters that have the highest occurrence.

For example encoding the string LEMMONS, E would be encoded as 101, whereas M would be encoded as 01 as it appears more often.

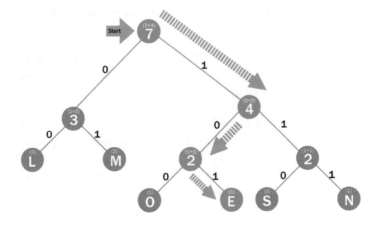

HVD stands for High Voltage Differential and is the logic signalling system originally defined in the SCSI-2 standard. HVD has a maximum logic voltage of 5V and uses a paired plus and minus signal level to reduce the effects of noise on the SCSI bus. It was functionally replaced by LVD (Low Voltage Differential) in the SCSI-3 variant of the standard. HVD and LVD SCSI are not directly compatible but can be interconnected by the use of a special adapter.

Hyperlink is a pointer from text or an image map to a page or other type of file on the world wide web. On web pages, hyperlinks are the primary way to navigate between pages and among web sites.

Hyperthreading is Intel's hardware technology that allows more than one thread to run on each CPU core. Each physical core on the CPU is split into virtual cores called threads and appear as separate physical CPUs to the operating system

HyperTransport is an industry standard high-speed, high-performance, point-to-point connection method for integrated circuits pioneered by AMD. It initially allowed for connection speeds of up to 6.4GBps.

Hz is short for Hertz, and is the standard unit of frequency named after Heinrich Rudolf Hertz. It is defined as the number cycles per second and is commonly used to measure radio frequencies, computer clock speeds and so on.

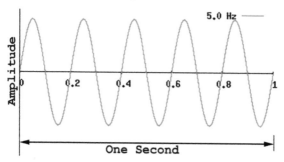

I

I/O stands for Input/Output and refers to data transfer from input devices such as a keyboard, mouse, or scanner, to and output device such as a printer or monitor.

I/O Address is the memory location for a particular device (disk drive, sound card, printer port, etc.). Two devices cannot share the same I/O address space.

IA-32 stands for Intel Architecture 32-bit. Intel's 32-bit architecture, also known as x86. IA-32 chips span the early 1990s Intel 486 series to the seventh-generation Intel Pentium 4 and AMD Athlon chips. See also IA-64.

IA-64 stands for Intel Architecture 64-bit and is a 64-bit architecture jointly developed by HP and Intel with IA-32 compatibility. IA-64 supports 32-bit and 64- bit environments, and provides compatibility with IA-32 systems.

IBM PC also know as IBM AT, or PC AT, was launched in 1984 by IBM. It had 256K of RAM, and an Intel 80286 running at 8 MHz, with MS-DOS 3.0 as its operating system

IANA stands for Internet Assigned Numbers Authority and oversees global IP address allocation, autonomous system number allocation, and root zone management in DNS.

IC stands for Integrated Circuit and is a small electronic component produced in or on a small slice of silicon called a wafer. Its name comes from the integration of transistors, resistors and capacitors on a single chip.

IDE is short for Integrated Device Electronics or Intelligent Drive Electronics and is a drive-interface specification for disk drives in which all the drive's control electronics are part of the drive itself, rather than on a separate adapter connecting the drive to the expansion bus. See EIDE and SCSI.

IDE is Short for Integrated Development Environment and is a software development tool containing a source code editor, compiler, and debugger.

IEEE stands for Institute of Electrical and Electronics Engineers and is a membership organisation that includes engineers, scientists and students in electronics and allied fields. The IEEE sets standards for computers and communications, such as IEEE 802 standards for Local Area Networks, 802.3 for ethernet, 802.11 for WiFi and 1394 for firewire.

iMac is an all in one computer developed by Apple intended for use at home, in schools, and small offices, and promoted as an easy-to-use, stylish computer

Image is a computerised representation of a picture or graphic.

Image Resolution is the fineness or coarseness of an image as it was digitised, measured in Dots Per Inch (DPI), typically from 72 to 400 DPI.

IMAP stands for Internet Message Access Protocol, an email protocol that allows you to directly manage your emails on the email server without having to download them to a mail client program first.

IMT-2000 stands for International Mobile Telecommunications 2000 and is a worldwide set of standards for the 3rd generation cellular communications.

Index is a pointer used to indicate a specific location.

Inheritance in computer programming is the feature of an object class to take on characteristics of its parent. Here we have a parent class called Person, and two child classes called Student and Staff. The child classes inherit all the attributes and methods of the parent classes. Child classes can include any additional attributes and methods that are not accessible from other classes.

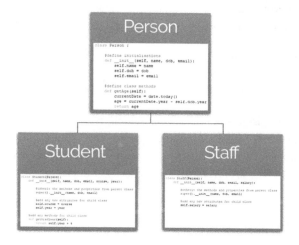

Inkjet is a printer technology where ink is fired onto the printer paper to form an image or character.

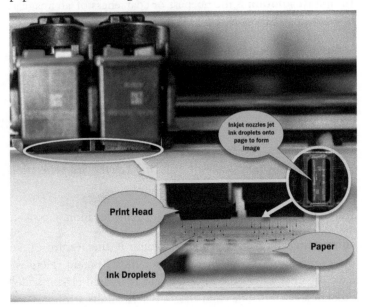

Instruction Cache is a temporary store of instructions usually on CPU allowing quick access.

Instruction Set is the complete set of instructions that can be executed by a processor.

Interactive Video is the combination of video and a computer program running under the control of the user where the viewer's decisions affect the way in which the video unfolds.

Interface is a shared link in which two or more separate components of a computer system can communicate and exchange information such as the various buses, storage devices such as IDE, SATA, SCSI, and other I/O devices.

Interframe Coding is a compression techniques that encodes the differences between frames of video.

Interlaced is a scheme used to render a video image by displaying alternate scan lines in two discrete fields.

Interleave refers to the arrangement of sequential data in a non sequential way to increase performance.

Interleave Factor is a technique used by older hard disk drives to arrange sectors in a non-contiguous way so as to reduce latency thereby increasing read/write performance. The interleave factor specifies the physical spacing between consecutive logical sectors.

Internal Drive is a drive mounted inside one of a computer's drive bays (or a hard disk on a card, which is installed in one of the computer's slots).

Internet is a global system of interconnected computer networks linked together using the TCP/IP protocol, and evolved from a research project to develop a robust, fault-tolerant communication network back in the 1960s, known as ARPANET. Today, you can connect to the internet in a variety of different ways. Many of today's Internet Service Providers offer a DSL, Cable or Fibre Optic connection to the internet, depending on where you are.

InterNIC stands for Internet Network Information Center and was the organization responsible for domain name and IP address allocations until 1998.

Intranet is usually a private network designed to share information, collaboration and various other computing services within an organisation

Interpreter is a translator that converts one high level language program statement into machine code at a time and then executes it, before moving onto the next statement. Python and Javascript are interpreted programming language.

Invar is a type of metal used in the shadow mask that provides more consistent images over time, by reducing warping of the shadow mask when bright images are displayed.

Inverse Kinematics is process of calculating the variable parameters needed to determine the motion of a robot or animated character to reach a position relative to the start. For example when building a robotic arm to perform a task, inverse kinematics can determine an appropriate joint configuration to move the arm to a specific position.

Ion is an atom or molecule that has a net electrical charge. A positive ion is called a cation (pronounced "cat-eye-on") as it has fewer electrons than protons, and a negative ion is called an anion (pronounced "an-eye-on") as it has more electrons than protons. In semiconductor manufacturing, ions are the source of chemical impurities that alter the conductivity of silicon.

iOS is a mobile operating system developed by Apple for their line of iPads and iPhones.

IP Address stands for Internet Protocol, a numerical address assigned to each device connected to a computer network. IPv4 defines an IP address as a 32-bit number divided into four 8 bit octets, and is usually expressed as a dotted decimal number each ranging from 1 to 254. Eg 192.168.1.2. IPv6 uses eight 16-bit hexadecimal numbers separated by a colon. Eg: fdaa:bbcc:ddee:0000:71a4:c9d5:57d4:ec99

IPC stands for Instructions Per Clock and is a measure of how many instructions a CPU is capable of executing in a single clock. Since different processor architectures have different

IPv4 stands for Internet Protocol Version 4. A numerical address assigned to each device connected to a computer network. IPv4 defines an IP address as a 32-bit number divided into four 8 bit octets, and is usually expressed as a dotted decimal number each ranging from 1 to 254. Eg:

192.168.1.2

IPv6 stands for Internet Protocol Version 6, a numerical address assigned to each device connected to a computer network. IPv6 uses eight 16-bit hexadecimal numbers separated by a colon. Eg:

An IPv6 address can be broken down into various parts to identify the site or organisation, network, and device.

IrDA stands for Infrared Data Association and is a standard for transmitting data via infrared light. IrDA ports enable the transfer of data between IrDA devices such as computers and printers without using a cable.

IRQ stands for Interrupt ReQuest and is a signal generated by a device to request processing time from the CPU. Each time a keyboard button is pressed or a character is printed to a screen, an IRQ is generated by the requesting device. IRQ signals are transmitted along IRQ lines which connect peripheral devices to a programmable interrupt controller, or PIC.

ISA stands for Industry Standard Architecture and is the architectural standard for the IBM XT (8-bit) and the IBM AT (16-bit) bus designs. In ISA systems, an adapter added by plugging the card into one of the 16-bit expansion slots enables expansion devices like network cards, video adapters and modems to send data to and receive data from the PC's CPU and memory 16 bits at a time. See also EISA.

ISDN stands for Integrated Services Digital Network and is the CCITT standard that defines a completely digital telephone/ telecommunications network which carries voice, data, and video over existing telephone network infrastructure. ISDN provides two 64 Kbit/s channels, which can be combined or used independently for both voice and data. It is designed to provide a single interface for hooking up a phone, fax machine, PC, etc.

ISO stands for International Standards Organisation and is an international body responsible for establishing and managing various standards committees and expert groups, including several image-compression standards.

ISO Image is an archive that contains an identical copy of an optical disk such as a CD or DVD. Nowadays ISO images are used for distributing large programs and operating systems as this allows all the files to be contained in one easily downloadable file. The ISO image can then be "burned" to a CD, DVD or Flash Drive.

Isochronous refers to processes where data must be delivered within certain time constraints. For example, multimedia streams require an isochronous transport mechanism to ensure that data is delivered as fast as it is displayed and to ensure that the audio is synchronised with the video. See Asynchronous and Synchronous.

ISP stands for Internet Service Provider and is a company that provides access to the Internet for a monthly fee. The ISP provides subscribers with the necessary hardware such as an ADSL modem and a user account. The modem usually connects to a telephone line allowing the user to browse and download from the WWW as well as send and receive e-mail.

Itanium is the brand name for the first product in Intel's IA-64 family of processors, formerly codenamed Merced.

ITU stands for International Telecommunications Union and is the United Nations agency for telecommunications. The ITU combines the standards- setting activities of the predecessor organisations formerly called the International Telegraph and Telephone Consultative Committee (CCITT) and the International Radio Consultative Committee (CCIR), being charged with establishing and co-ordinating standards for electronic communications worldwide.

iTunes is a now deprecated media player app developed by Apple that allowed users to purchase and download music. iTunes was later split into the music app, podcasts app and the TV app.

J

Jack is the hole in which a plug is inserted. For example, audio jack.

Jaggies also known as Aliasing. A term for the jagged visual appearance of lines and shapes in raster pictures that results from producing graphics on a grid format. This effect can be reduced by increasing the sample rate in scan conversion.

Java is an object oriented programming language originally developed by Sun Microsystems and used in embedded devices, mobile phones, supercomputers and web applications on the internet.

JavaScript is a scripting language for web pages which allows simple interactivity to be built into a page.

JEDEC is an organisation that establishes standards for memory operation, features, and packaging.

Jitter is the interference that occurs causing a shimmering effect that results in lines and characters to lose their focus. It can occur when a TFT panel's clock and phase aren't synchronised.

Joliet endorsed my Microsoft, an extension to the ISO 9660 specification for content on a CD-ROM. Joliet allows file names of up to 64 characters in length (including spaces) as well as the use of unicode characters in file names.

JPEG stands for Joint Photographic Experts Group and is a still-image compression method commonly used to store digital photographs. JPEG uses a Discrete Cosine Transfer algorithm to reduce the amount of data necessary to represent digital images allowing a trade off between image quality and size.

High Compression   **Low Compression**

Jumper is a small metal block with plastic covered handles for enabling or disabling specific functions on a motherboard or expansion card.

Just-Noticeable Difference In the CIELAB colour model, a difference in hue, chroma, or intensity, or some combination of all three, that is apparent to a trained observer under ideal lighting conditions. A just-noticeable difference is a change of 1; a change of 5 is apparent to most people most of the time.

K

K56flex is a protocol jointly developed by Lucent Technologies and Rockwell International Corp to achieve 56 Kbit/s modem transmissions over ordinary phone lines. K56flex allows downloads at up to 56 Kbit/s; uploads are limited to the normal V.34 speed of 33.6 Kbit/s. See also X2.

KB stands for Kilobyte, a unit of data storage equivalent to 1000 bytes. A Kibibyte is 1024 bytes. See KiB.

Kbit is short for Kilobit and is a unit of measure consisting of 1000 bits. The unit often used in expressions of data transmission capacity.

Kbit/s is short for Kilobits Per Second (or Kbps) and is a measure of data transfer speed. Note that 1 Kbit/s is 1,000 bits per second. Data transfer rates are measured using the decimal meaning of K whereas data storage is measured using the powers-of-2 meaning of K.

Kbps short for Kilobits per second. Note lowercase 'b'.

KBps short for Kilobytes per second, a performance measure used for mass storage devices and memory systems. Note uppercase 'B'.

Kernel is the program at the core of an operating system that has complete control of the system and is primarily responsible for memory and process management, device/hardware control and system calls. Example the linux kernel.

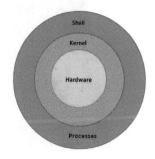

Kerning is the process of adjusting the spacing between two individual font characters.

Kerr Effect is a change in rotation of light reflected off a magnetic field. The polarity of a magneto-optic bit causes the laser to shift one degree clockwise or counter clockwise.

Keyframe is a marker on a timeline which marks the beginning or end of a transition or animation - the computer calculates the frames in between to create a smooth effect. Also in video compression algorithms, a keyframe is a frame in the video that contains the complete picture, the rest of the frames contain the changes from the previous frame. This means that only small pieces of information need to be stored about each frame in order for the whole frame to be reconstructed at playback. See Delta Frame.

Keys are notches carved into the contact edge of a memory module (DRAM DIMM) that prevent them from being plugged into an incompatible system.

Keystone Distortion is a type of geometric distortion where the vertical edges of an image slant inwards towards the top horizontal edge.

KHz is short for KiloHertz and is a measure of frequency equal to 1000 hertz. See Hz.

KiB stands for Kibibyte and is a unit of measure consisting of 1024 bytes. See also MiB, GiB and TiB.

Kilobyte (KB) derived from the Standards Insitute prefix kilo meaning 1000, a unit of information or computer storage. Abbreviations for kilobyte include KB, kB, Kbyte, and kbyte.

Knowledge Base is a large collection of articles and documents maintained by a company as part of their customer support to assist customers with problems. See FAQ.

L

LAN is a small network contained on a single site or building. As you can see in the diagram below, the network covers a small area. The computers could be split up into different offices or all in one room and can all access resources served from the file server and use internet services provided by the router.

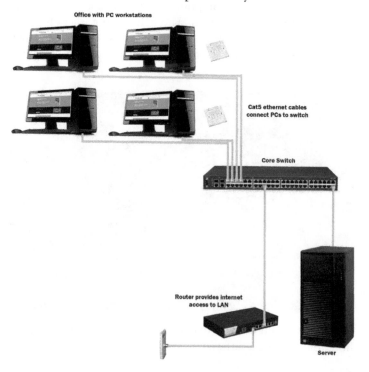

Office with PC workstations

Cat5 ethernet cables connect PCs to switch

Core Switch

Router provides internet access to LAN

Server

All the machines on the network are connected together with Cat5 cable and a switch.

Landing Zone is the non-data area set-aside on a hard drive platter for the heads to rest when the system powers down.

LAPM stands for Link Access Procedure For Modems and is one of the two protocols specified by V.42. LAPM provides error control when a modem is communicating with another modem that supports LAPM.

Laser Disc is an obsolete optical disk that was used for full-motion video. In the 1970s, various videodisc systems were introduced, but only the Philips LaserVision survived. Superseded by DVD in 2001.

Laser Printer is a type of printer that utilises a laser beam to produce an image on a drum. The light of the laser alters the electrical charge on the drum wherever it hits. The drum is then rolled through a reservoir of toner, which is picked up by the charged portions

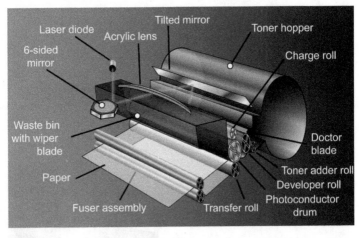

Latch is a circuit element that stores a given value on its output until told to store a different value.

Latency is the time between initiating a request for data and the beginning of the actual data transfer. For example, the average latency of a hard disk drive is easily calculated from the spindle speed, as the time for half a rotation. In communications, network latency is the delay introduced when a packet is momentarily stored, analysed and then forwarded.

Lathing is creating a 3-D surface by rotating a 2-D spline around an axis.

LBA is short for Logical Block Addressing and is the scheme by which the BIOS passes an operating system request for a given sector to a modern hard drive.

LCD stands for Liquid Crystal Display and is a display technology that uses polarising light filters and liquid crystal cells to produce an on a screen.

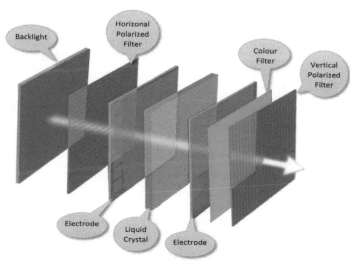

LCD Printer is similar to a laser printer but instead of using a laser to create an image on the drum, the printer shines a light through an LCD panel. Individual pixels in the panel either let the light pass or block it to create the image on the print drum.

LCOS stands for Liquid Crystal on Silicon and is a liquid crystal layer on top of a pixelated, highly-reflective substrate. Below the substrate is a backplane that includes the electronics to drive the pixels. The backplane and liquid crystals are combined into a panel and packaged for use in a projection subsystem or "light engine."

LED stands for Light Emitting Diode and is a display technology that uses a semiconductor diodes that emits light 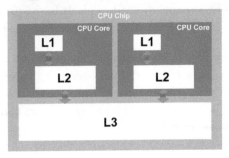 when charged. LEDs are usually red. It was the first digital watch display, but was superseded by LCD, which uses less power.

LED Printer is an electro-photographic printer similar to a laser printer except it uses a matrix of LEDs as its light source instead of a laser. The LED matrix bar pulse-flashes across the width of the page to create an image on the print drum.

Legacy is a term used to describe an application, architecture, protocol, system or system component that has been in existence for a long time.

LEP stands for Light-Emitting Polymer and is a display technology in which plastics are made to conduct electricity and, under certain conditions, emit light.

Level 1 Cache is the cache that built into the processor core itself and is the fastest cache. Also referred to as primary cache or internal cache.

Level 2 Cache is a fast memory bank located on the processor core usually slower but bigger than the Level 1 Cache. Also referred to as secondary cache and external cache.

Level 3 Cache is memory bank located outside the processor core which is bigger and often shared between cores.

LFB stands for Linear Frame Buffer and is a buffer organised in a linear fashion, so that a single address increment can be used to step from one pixel to the pixel below it in the next scan line in the frame buffer.

LGA775 is short for Land Grid Array 775 and is Intel's proprietary CPU interface introduced in the summer of 2004. Similar to a pin grid array (PGA), the connection between LGA775 chip packaging and the processor chip is via an array of solder bumps rather than pins. Also referred to as Socket T.

LIFO stands for Last In First Out and is a queuing method in which the next item to be retrieved is the item most recently placed in the queue. See also FIFO.

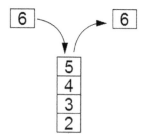

Lighting is an effect in 3D graphics used to simulate light in a scene.

Line Art is a type of graphic consisting entirely of lines, without any shading.

Line Noise is a random signal disturbance that sometimes occurs over a telephone line. Noise can disrupt communications and corrupt the transmitted data. The ratio of the usable signal to unusable noise on a communications link is referred to as the signal-to-noise ratio. Fibre optic cables are far less susceptible to noise than metal wire cables.

Linux is a free, open source operating system originally developed by Linus Torvalds, similar to the Unix operating system. Linux has evolved to run on a wide variety of hardware from phones to PCs to supercomputers and is typically packaged in a Linux distribution. There are various distributions available such as Ubuntu, Redhat, SuSE, Centos, Raspbian to name a few.

Local Bus is a bus which co-exists with the main bus and connects the processor itself to the main memory. PCI-Express is now the standard local bus architecture, having replaced the older incarnations.

Local Loop are the lines between a customer and the telephone company's central office, often called the last mile. Local loops often use copper cables.

Localhost is the address used to point to the local computer on a network. The IP address is 127.0.0.1, also known as a loopback address.

Logic Gate is an electronic device made up of transistors that implement Boolean logic operations on a circuit board. Transistors make up logic gates which make up circuits, and circuits make up electronic systems.

Here below we have AND, NOT, OR, NAND, NOR, XOR gates.

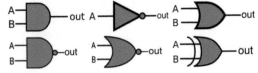

Look Ahead is a technique used for buffering data into cache RAM by reading subsequent blocks in advance to anticipate the next request for data. The look ahead technique speeds up disk access of sequential blocks of data.

Loop Qualification is this is a test done by the phone company to make sure the customer is within the maximum ISDN distance of 18,000 feet from the central office that services that customer.

Loopback Address is 127.0.0.1 or localhost used to identify the local machine on a network. See localhost.

Loopback Test is a diagnostic test where characters that are sent to the modem are immediately sent back from the modem so the computer can compare the characters sent with the characters received.

Lossless is a compression method for compressing data without losing any information such as GIF or Zip file.

Lossy is a compression method for compressing data by discarding unnecessary data. This results in much smaller file sizes than with lossless compression, but at the expense of some artefacts. JPEG image files use lossy compression.

Low Profile describes drives built to the 3.5in form factor, which are only 1in high. The standard form factor drives are 1.625in high.

Low-Level Formatting is the process often completed by a drive manufacturer to initiate a hard disk drive and prepare it for storing data. The low level format creates tracks and sectors on the surface of the disk. The operating system can then use a high level format to create the file system such as NTFS or FAT32 so users can store data and applications.

LPT1 was the first parallel or printer port on a PC.

LPX is a motherboard form factor which allows for smaller cases used in some desktop model PCs. The distinguishing characteristic of LPX is that expansion boards are inserted into a riser that contains several slots and are therefore parallel, rather than perpendicular, to the motherboard.

LSI stands for Large Scale Integration and refers to the placement of thousands (between 3,000 and 100,000) of electronic components on a single integrated circuit. VLSI (Very Large Scale Integration) is between 100,000 and one million transistors on a chip.

Lumen is a measure of brightness ie the amount of visible light emitted by a light source. Higher the lumen the brighter the light.

Luminance is the amount of light intensity; one of the three image characteristics coded in composite television (represented by the letter Y). May be measured in lux or foot-candles. Also referred to as Intensity.

LVD stands for Low Voltage Differential and is a high-speed, long-distance digital interface for serial communication over copper cable.

LZW stands for Lempel-Zif-Welch and is a data compression technique developed in 1977 by J. Ziv and A Lempel widely used in various hardware and software products such as data transmission, as well as in GIF and TIFF image files.

M

M.2 is a form factor for internal expansion cards used to mount internal devices such as WiFi cards and SSD drives. They are small and have a long rectangular appearance. Here's an M.2 SSD drive.

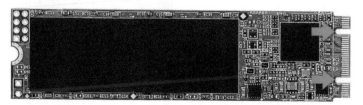

The card's connectors are keyed depending on which interface they're compatible with. Here's a summary.

Connector Key	Card Measurements (mm)	Interface	Uses
A	1630, 2230, 3030	PCIe x2, USB 2.0	Wi-Fi and Bluetooth cards
B	2230, 2242, 2260, 2280, 3042, 22110	PCIe x2, SATA, USB 2.0, USB 3.0	SATA and PCIe x2 SSDs
M	2242, 2260, 2280, 22110	PCIe x4, SATA	PCIe x4 SSDs, NVMe

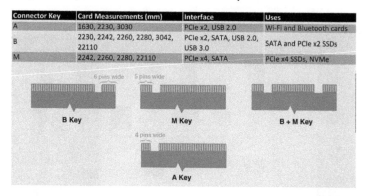

MAC stands for Medium Access Control and is a protocol found on the data link layer of the OSI 7 layer Model, responsible for moving data frames from one Network Interface Card (NIC) to another.

MAC address or media access control address is a unique identifier permanently allocated to a hardware device on a network.

Macintosh first introduced by Apple in 1984, marked a breakthrough in personal computer technology, featuring a graphical user interface (GUI) that utilised windows, icons and a mouse for navigation.

The success of the Macintosh GUI led a new age of graphics-based applications and operating systems. Microsoft's subsequent Windows interface copied many features from the Macintosh.

MacOS is a proprietary operating system developed by Apple for its Macintosh line of personal computers and laptops.

MacOS is build on a UNIX kernel with a graphic user interface called Aqua which features a dock for launching apps, a finder for opening files, and a dashboard for small handy applets called widgets.

Main Memory also known as RAM or primary storage, is the main data storage location where the microprocessor fetches, executes and stores instructions as well as any data required by the instruction..

MAN is short for Metropolitan Area Network. A network spanning a city for example, a university campus.

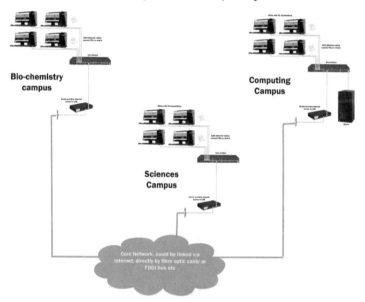

Manual Dialling is dialling a remote modem from a telephone connected to the modem. This is in contrast to automatic dialling, where the modem dials the number.

MAPI is short for Messaging Application Programming Interface and is an API developed by Microsoft and other computer vendors that provides Windows applications with an implementation independent interface to various messaging systems.

Mapping is placing an image on or around an object so that the image is like the object's skin.

Mask are used like stencils in the chip making process. When used with the UV light, masks create the various circuit patterns on each layer of the microprocessor. Also used to describe the information in the alpha channel of a graphic that determines how effects are rendered.

MB stands for Megabyte and is a unit of data storage equivalent to 1 million bytes (1,048,576 bytes).

Mbit/s is short for Megabits Per Second (or Mbps) and is a measure of data transfer speed. Note that 1 Mbit/s is 1 million bits per second. Data transfer rates are measured using the decimal meaning of M whereas data storage is measured using the powers-of-2 meaning of M.

MBR is short for Master Boot Record, and is the first sector of a disk that identifies where an operating system is located, and how it is booted.

MCA stands for Micro Channel Architecture and is a 32-bit bus architecture introduced by IBM for their PS/2 series microcomputers. Incompatible with original PC/AT (ISA) architecture.

MCI stands for Media Control Interface and is a platform-independent multimedia specification published by Microsoft Corporation and others in 1990 to provide a consistent way to control devices such video playback units.

Media is any component used to store data such as a tape, hard disk, flash drive, DVD, or CD.

Megabyte derived from the Standards Insitute prefix mega, meaning a million is a unit of computer storage that the equals one million bytes.

Memory Bank is a logical unit of memory in a computer. For example, a 64-bit CPU requires memory banks that provide 64bits of information at a time. A bank can consist of one or more memory modules.

Memory Controller is an essential component that oversees the movement of data into and from main memory.

Memory Cycle is the minimum amount of time required for a memory chip to complete a cycle such as read, write, read/write, or read/modify/write.

MEMS is short for Micro-electromechanical systems and is the name for technology that embeds mechanical devices such as fluid sensors, mirrors, actuators, pressure and temperature sensors, vibration sensors and valves in semiconductor chips. MEMS combine many disciplines, including physics, bioinformatics, biochemistry, electrical engineering, optics and electronics.

Mesh Model is a graphical model with a mesh surface constructed from polygons. The polygons in a mesh are described by the graphics system as solid faces, rather than as hollow polygons, as is the case with wireframe models. Separate portions of mesh that make up the model are called polygon mesh and quadrilateral mesh.

Metals such as aluminium and copper are used to conduct the electricity throughout the microprocessor. Gold is also used to connect the actual chip to its package.

Mflops short for Megaflops and is 1 million floating-point instructions per second.

MFM stands for Modified Frequency Modulation and is the data storage system used by floppy disk drives and older early hard disk drives. Had twice the capacity of the earlier FM method but was slower than the competing RLL scheme.

MHz short for Megahertz and is a measurement of frequency in millions of cycles per second.

MiB stands for Mebibyte and is a unit of data storage consisting of 1024KiB or 1,048,576 bytes.

Microcode is the lowest-level instructions that directly control a microprocessor. A single machine-language instruction typically translates into several microcode instructions. In modern PC microprocessors, the microcode is hard-wired and can't be modified.

Microdrive is an ultra-miniature hard disk technology from IBM that uses a single one-inch diameter platter to provide either 170MB or 340MB storage capacity and either one or two GMR heads, the Microdrive is built into a Type II CompactFlash form factor.

Micron µm is a unit of measure equivalent to one-millionth of a metre; synonymous with micrometre.

Microsecond µs is one millionth of a second (.000001 sec.).

Mid Span Repeater is a device that amplifies the signal coming or going to the central office. This device is necessary for ISDN service if you are outside the 18,000 feet distance requirement from the central office.

MIDI stands for Musical Instrument Digital Interface and is a specification that standardises the interface between computers and digital devices that simulate musical instruments. Instead of transmitting large digitised sound samples, the MIDI synthesiser sends commands just a few bytes in length containing information such as instrument, note pitch, duration, volume, attack, and decay. Each channel of a MIDI synthesiser corresponds to a different instrument called a "voice".

MIDI Mapper is a windows multimedia translator for MIDI hardware and software.

Midtones are the parts of an image that are in the middle of the tonal range, halfway between the lightest and the darkest tones.

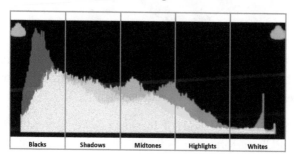

Millisecond One thousandth of a second – 0.001 sec.

MIME stands for Multi-purpose Internet Mail Extension and is the format used for transmitting files across the Internet. Since email messages are designed for text data, this format converts the non text data into a text-based format. Often used for encoding email attachments.

MiniDisc or MD for short is a compact digital audio disc from Sony that comes in read-only and rewritable versions. Introduced in late 1993, the MiniDisc has been popular in Japan. The read-only 2.5in disc stores 140MB compared to 650MB on a CD, but holds  the same 74 minutes worth of music due to Sony's Adaptive Transform Acoustic Coding (ATRAC) compression scheme, which eliminates inaudible portions of the signal.

MiniDVD a smaller DVD disk 8 centimetres in diameter and usually holds 1.4GB - 2.8GB of data.

Mip Mapping is a sophisticated texturing technique to ensure that 3D objects gain detail smoothly when approaching or receding. This is typically produced in two ways; per-triangle (faster) or per pixel (more accurate).

MIPS stands for Millions of Instructions Per Second and refers to a CPU's performance. Is the benchmark for comparing CPU performance.

Mission Control is a feature native to MacOS that shows every application you have open and allows you to add and manage virtual desktops. You can open mission control by pressing control and the up arrow.

Mixed-Signal Device collects analogue signals and converts them into digital data to be processed. Once a DSP processes and compresses the digital data, a mixed-signal device decompresses, transmits and displays the digital data as either digital or analogue signals.

MMO is Intel's pop-out CPU packaging designed for mobile processors which includes an integrated L2 cache, introduced with Mobile MMX processor launched in early 1998.

MMX stands for MultiMedia eXtensions and was incorporated into Intel's Pentium processor to provide additional instructions designed specifically for processing multimedia data more efficiently. Codenamed P55C.

MNOS stands for Metal Nitride Oxide Semiconductor and is the technology used for EAROMs (Electrically Alterable ROMs); not to be confused with NMOS.

MNP stands for Microcom Networking Protocol and is a series of standards, running from MNP Class 1 to MNP Class 10, designed to improve communications between modems but now superseded by LAPM. They do not stand alone, but operate in conjunction with other modem standards.

Modelling is the process of creating 3-D objects.

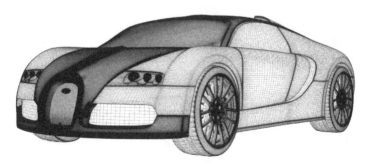

Modem is short for MOdulator/DEModulator and is a device that converts digital data into an analogue signal that can be sent across a telephone line (modulation). It also converts the analogue signal it receives from the telephone line, back into digital information (demodulation).

Analog Phone Line

Modes specific frequencies at which the monitor (and/or computer) can display text or graphical information. Most monitors today support several frequencies. This is called multi-frequency or multi-scanning, and it ensures that the monitor will perform with a variety of computers and applications.

Modulation is converting a data stream into sounds to be sent down a phone line. The opposite is demodulation. See also Modem, PM, FM, AM.

Moir is a noticeable pattern of interference, often perceived as flickering. For example, a TV image of someone wearing a herringbone jacket can cause the effect. In images of closely spaced lines or other finely detailed patterns, these ripples or waves can appear on colour monitors as well as in scanned images.

Mojave is the fifteenth major release of macOS for Macintosh Computers. Mojave introduced new features such as Continuity Camera, Dark Mode, Desktop Stacks and Dynamic Desktops.

Molex is a plastic connector with cylindrical pins often used to supply power to components such as disk drives.

Moore's Law is Gordon Moore's famous prediction that the number of transistors per integrated circuit would double every 18 months..

MOPS stands for Millions of Operations Per Second.

Morph short for metamorphosing, morphing refers to an animation technique in which one image is gradually turned into another.

MOS stands for Metal-Oxide-Semiconductor and are the layers used to create a semiconductor circuit. A thin insulating layer of oxide is deposited on the surface of the wafer. Then a highly conductive layer of tungsten silicide is placed over the top of the oxide dielectric.

Motherboard a large circuit board found in desktop and laptop computer systems that house the majority of the electronics required by the computer such as memory, CPU, as well as various expansions slots and drive interfaces..

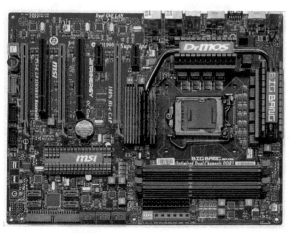

Motion Video is video that displays real motion by displaying a sequence of images (called frames) rapidly enough that the eyes see a continuously moving picture.

Motion-JPEG is a derivative of JPEG that includes some keyframe based compression to make it suitable for video.

MP stands for Multilink PPP and is a protocol that allows a device to use two PPP communications ports as if they were a single port of greater bandwidth.

MP3 is short for MPEG Audio Layer-3 and is an audio compression format often used to compress music, that employs a lossy compression technique, along with psycho acoustic compression - meaning audio beyond human hearing is removed, or a quiet sound when followed by a loud sound.

MP4 is short for MPEG-4 part 14 and is video container format that encloses a video stream usually encoded using H264/5, and an audio stream encoded using MP3 or AAC. The MP4 format is commonly used for streaming video on the Internet and is supported by a wide range of video playback apps, hardware devices, and services.

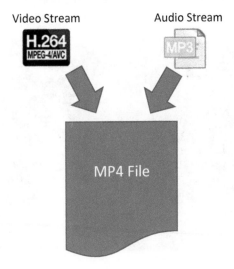

MPEG stands for Moving Picture Experts Group and is a standards committee, supported by ISO, formed to establish uniform methodologies and algorithms for digital audio and video compression.

MPEG 1 Audio defined three different coding schemes for digitized audio, called Layers I, II, and III, utilizing psychoacoustics to reduce the amount of data. Layer I commonly known as MP1 encodes data at bit rates of 32 up to 448 Kbps and sampling frequencies of 32, 44.1 and 48 kHz. Layer II known as MP2, provides a higher compression efficiency with a sampling frequency of 192 to 256 Kbps for near CD quality audio. Layer III commonly known as MP3 provides a higher compression efficiency than Layer I & II, and can compress CD quality audio.

MPEG-1 Video standard was a video compression standard used in VideoCDs. MPEG-1 video offered resolutions of up to 352 × 240 at 29.97 fps and 352 × 288 at 25 fps with 24-bit colour and CD quality sound.

MPEG-2 Video standard offers resolutions of 720× 480 and 1280×720 at 60 fps, with full CD-quality audio. This is sufficient for all the major TV standards, including NTSC, and even HDTV. MPEG-2 is used by DVD-ROMs and is capable of compressing a 2 hour video into a few gigabytes.

MPEG-4 Video is a video compression method from the MPEG group, that was especially designed for low-bandwidth video/audio encoding purposes (less than 1.5Mbps). Not to be confused with MP4.

MPR2 provides reduced electrostatic and electromagnetic emissions. MPR 1990, or MPR2, is a standard defined to measure emissions from devices such as monitors.

MTBF is short for Mean Time Between Failure, the average time a specific component is expected to work without failure.

MTTR is short for Mean Time To Repair: the average time to repair a specific component.

Multi Mode fibre uses multiple light rays (or modes) through a 62.5 or 50 micron cable and can transmit up to 2 km.

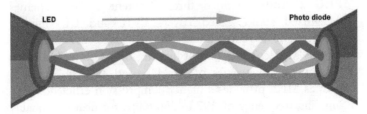

Here's a multimode ST patch cable. Notice the cables come in pairs. This is because the light signals travel in only one direction, so you need 1 cable to transmit, and one to receive.

Multi-Frequency is a monitor's ability to change resolution or refresh rate when signalled by a video adapter. Graphics adapters have the ability to "tell" a monitor to use various display resolutions and refresh rates. If the resolution or refresh rate is within a monitor's scanning range, multi-frequency monitors adjust to the resolutions and refresh rates "ordered" by the video adapter. Also known as multi-scanning. See also Modes.

Multilevel Feedback Queueing is a process scheduling system where each processes enters on the high priority queue. If a process uses too much CPU time, it is moved down to a lower-priority queue.

Processes on the lower queues are not serviced until all processes in the queues above are empty. The bottom queue uses a round robin scheduling scheme.

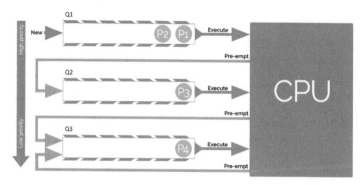

Multimedia refers to the delivery of information that combines different content formats (motion video, audio, still images, graphics, animation, text, etc.).

Multiplexer is a device that integrates serial digital waveforms into a single channel by partitioning the inputted data into segments and combining them together into a bitstream.

Multiprocessing is a single computer system with more than one physical CPU.

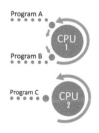

Multiscan is a monitor that can display many different resolutions. A single-scan monitor can only display a particular resolution.

Multitasking is the concurrent execution of multiple tasks, programs or processes. Pre-emptive multitasking uses a scheduling system where each running process receives a slice of time from the CPU. When it's time expires, the process is interrupted.

Multithreading is multiple concurrent threads of execution within a single application.

Multi-Timbral is the number of simultaneous instruments a synthesiser can play.

Munsell Colour System is a system consisting of over 3 million observations of what people perceive to be like differences in hue, chroma, and intensity. The participants chose the samples they perceived to have like differences.

MX Record is a record on a DNS server that points to the mail server responsible for dealing with email messages sent to a domain.

MySQL pronounced "My Sequel", or "My S.Q.L.", is an open-source relational database management system commonly used in web development. Many content management systems such as WordPress, Joomla, and Drupal use a MySQL database to store website data.

N

Nanometre nm: one thousand millionth of a metre.

Nanosecond ns: one thousand-millionths of a second of a second (.000000001 sec.). Light travels approximately 8 inches in 1 nanosecond.

Napster was created in 1999 by Shawn Fanning and was a pioneering peer-to-peer file sharing system that gave users access to one each other's MP3 files to the dismay of the Recording Industry Association of America.

NAS Drive sometimes called Network Attached Storage, is a device containing hard drives that connects to a network allowing users to share a data store between all the machines that are connected.

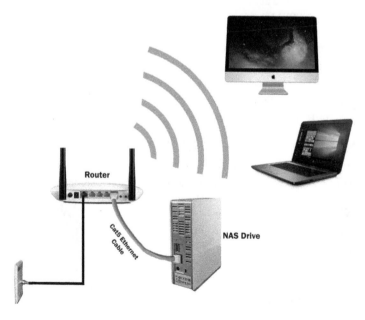

NCQ stands for Native Command Queuing and is a technology designed to increase performance of SATA hard disks by allowing the disk firmware to internally optimise the order in which read and write commands are executed. For NCQ to be enabled, it must be supported and turned on in the SATA controller driver and in the hard drive itself.

NetBEUI stands for NetBIOS Extended User Interface, and was a networking protocol developed by IBM and Microsoft in 1985 for local area networks with up to 200 stations.

NetBIOS stands for Network Basic Input/Output System, was an interface developed by IBM in the 80s that allowed computers and devices to communicate over a network.

NetBIOS Name is a unique name give to a machine on a network.

Network is a group of two or more computer systems linked together. There are many types of computer networks, including LANs and WANs.

Network Address Translation (NAT) maps multiple private IP addresses to a public IP on the router in order to provide Internet access to the private hosts. NAT takes outbound packets from clients on the private network and translates the private IP into the public IP

Nginx, pronouned "engine-ex", is a free, open-source server application that powers web servers across the internet. Nginx usually runs on a linux distribution similar to Apache.

NIC is short for Network Interface Card and is a card installed in a computer system to provides network communication capabilities to and from that computer.

Nit is a unit of luminance equal to one candlepower measured at a distance of 1m over an area of 1 square metre.

NLE stands for Non-Linear Editing and refers to the process of manipulating digitised video on a computer using specialised software such as Adobe Premiere, iMovie or Final Cut. The video clips can be cut, pasted and copied anywhere in the timeline of the project.

NLX is an Intel-designed motherboard form factor. It features a number of improvements over the ATX design providing support for new technologies such as AGP and allows easier access to motherboard components.

NMI stands for NonMaskable Interrupt and is a high-priority interrupt used to report malfunctions such as parity, bus and math co-processor errors.

NMOS stands for N-channel Metal Oxide Semiconductor and pertains to MOS devices constructed on a P-type substrate in which electrons flow between N-type source and drain contacts. NMOS devices are typically two to three times faster than PMOS devices.

Node is an endpoint of a network connection or a junction common to two or more lines in a network. Nodes can be processors, controllers, or workstations. The term is often used generically to refer to any entity that can access a network, and is frequently used interchangeably with device.

Noise is interference (or static) that disrupts the integrity of signals on communications lines. Noise can come from a variety of sources, including radio waves, nearby electrical wires, lightning, and bad connections. Noise is an analogue problem; once a signal is digitised, it is relatively immune to noise.

Non-Volatile Memory are types of memory that retain their contents when power is turned off. ROMs, PROMs, EPROMs and flash memory are examples. Sometimes the term refers to memory that is inherently volatile, but maintains its content because it is connected to a battery at all times, such as CMOS memory and to storage systems, such as hard disks.

North Bridge connects the CPU to the RAM and the PCI Express Graphics Card.

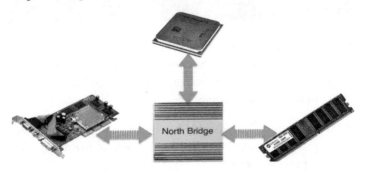

NOS stands for Network Operating System and is an operating system that include special functions for connecting computers and devices into a network. Some operating systems such as Windows and MacOS have networking functions built in. The term NOS is reserved for software that enhances a basic operating system by adding networking features.

NOT Gate has just one input. The NOT gate simply negates the input. So if the input is 1, the output is 0.

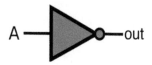

The truth table would be

A	Output
0	1
1	0

NTFS stands for New Technology File System, and is the file system native to Microsoft Windows. NTFS offers performance, compression, security, and the ability to handle large volumes and file sizes.

NTFS Permissions on the NTFS file system, is a set of permissions on a resource, file or folder that determine the access granted to a particular user. For example a user could have read only access to a shared folder, and full control of their own files.

NTSC stands for National Television Standards Committee and is the industry group that formulated the standards for American television. An NTSC signal is a composite video signal used by televisions and VCRs in North America and some other parts of the world. The NTSC system uses 525 lines per frame, a field frequency of 60 Hz, a 30-frame per second update rate, and the YIQ colour space. Modern NTSC encoders and decoders may also use the YUV colour space.

NURBS stands for Nonuniform Rational B-Spline and is a type of spline that can represent more complex shapes than a Bezier spline.

NVMe stands for Non-Volatile Memory Express and is a high-speed storage protocol using PCI express (x4) that was designed especially for SSDs. Drives that support this protocol have only one notch on the M.2 card connector (Key M).

NX stands for "No Execute" and is a joint venture hardware/software mechanism designed to defend against buffer overruns and consequent vulnerability to virus attack.

O

Object Oriented Programming, or OOP is a programming language that uses objects which contain data and code to develop software, rather than simply using functions and logic. Eg C++

OCR is short for Optical Character Recognition and is the electronic conversion of written or typed text into machine encoded text. Once converted the text can be edited.

ODBC short for Open Database Connectivity, and is a standard API that allows access to various database management programs such as DBASE, Microsoft Access, and Oracle using a common interface independent of the database file format. Using ODBC, you can write an application that uses the same code to read records from a DBASE file or a Microsoft Access Database

OEM is short for Original Equipment Manufacturer, and is a manufacturer that builds systems or components that are used in another company's end product. For example, when a PC-manufacturing company builds a PC or laptop they provide an operating system such as Microsoft Windows to the end-user. In this case, Microsoft is the OEM.

Off-Hook is a condition of a telephone line that corresponds to picking up the telephone receiver. A modem creates an off-hook condition when it tries to communicate on a telephone line.

OFTEL is the UK government regulator for telecommunications, first established in the 1980s to oversee the introduction of competition in a market dominated by British Telecom.

OLE stands for Object Linking and Embedding and is an industry-standard method for inserting an object into a document. The document retains a connection, or link, with its original program so that double-clicking on the object in the document opens the object's original program. See also DLL.

OLED short for Organic Light-Emitting Diode and is a display device that uses sandwich carbon-based films between two charged electrodes - a metallic cathode and a transparent anode. The organic films consist of a hole-injection layer, a hole-transport layer, an emissive layer and an electron-transport layer.

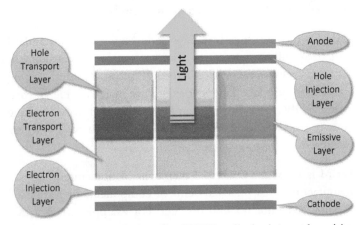

When voltage is applied to the OLED cell, the injected positive and negative charges recombine in the emissive layer and create electro luminescent light.

OneDrive is a file hosting and synchronization service developed by Microsoft that allow users to browse, view and organize files stored on their cloud storage space. OneDrive is integrated into Windows 10, with apps available for Android, iOS, as well as Xbox.

On-Hook is the condition of a telephone line that corresponds to hanging up the telephone receiver. A modem creates an on-hook condition to break its connection to a telephone line.

On-Line Mode is one of the two operating modes of the modem, also called data mode. In on-line mode, the modem interprets all information sent to it as data. The only exception is the escape sequence (normally "+++"), which returns the modem to command mode without breaking the connection.

OpenGL stands for Open Graphics Library and is a standardised cross platform API for rendering 2D and 3D graphics, often used in computer games and virtual reality.

Operating System or simply OS, is the software that controls the overall operation of a computer system, including such tasks as memory allocation, input and output distribution, interrupt processing, and job scheduling. The OS also provides a user interface for the user to interact such as GUI or CLI. MacOS, Windows, ChromeOS, iPadOS, iOS, Android and linux are common examples of operating systems.

Option is a key on a Mac keyboard, sometimes called the ALT key.

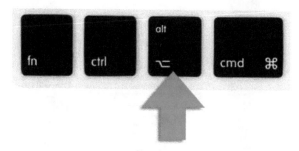

OR Gate has two inputs. An OR gates require either one or both inputs to be 1 for the output to be 1.

A	B	Output
0	0	0
0	1	1
1	0	1
1	1	1

OSI

OSI stands for Open System Interconnection and is an ISO standard for worldwide communications that defines a framework for implementing network protocols in seven layers. Information is passed down through the layers until it is transmitted across the network, where it is passed back up the stack to the application at the remote end.

OSI 7 Layer Model is a conceptual framework used to describe the functions of a computer network and is split into seven different layers: Physical, Data Link, Network, Transport, Session, Presentation, and Application. Each layer handles a different part of the communication.

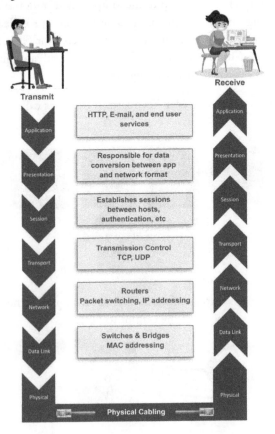

Overclock is to run a CPU or memory chip faster than its rated speed.

OverDrive is a distributor of eBooks, audiobooks, online magazines, and streaming video titles.

Overflow is a numerical answer that is too big for the allowed space to store

Overhead refers to the processing time required by the controller, host adapter, or drive prior to the execution of a command. Lower command overhead yields higher drive performance. Disk overhead refers to the space required for non- data information such as location and timing. Disk overhead often accounts for about ten percent of drive capacity. Lower disk overhead yields greater disk capacity.

Overlay is the ability to superimpose computer graphics over a live or recorded video signal and store the resulting video image on videotape. It is often used to add titles to videotape.

Overrun is the condition occurring when data is transmitted to a receiving device at a rate that's too fast for it to handle. See also Underrun and Flow Control.

Overscan is a condition that exists when a created image is larger than the visible portion of the display. Overscan helps relegate the relatively fuzzy perimeter of a CRT image to portions of the screen that are out of sight, and the overscan may disappear over time anyway. On the other hand, monitors with excessive overscan can lose icons and text at the edges of the display.

Overwrite is to write data over data already stored in a memory location.

P

P5 is Intel's codename for the original 60/66MHz Pentiums introduced in 1993. Subsequent faster clock-speed chips were referred to as P54 and the MMX version as P55.

P6 is Intel's codename for the Pentium Pro, which is optimised for 32-bit applications. The P6 generation includes the Pentium Pro and Pentium II.

PABX stands for Private Automatic Branch eXchange and is an in-house telephone switching system that interconnects telephone extensions to each other, as well as to the outside telephone network. Modern PBXs use all-digital methods for switching and can often handle digital terminals and telephones along with analogue telephones.

Packet is a basic unit of communication on a packet switched network that includes a header containing control information such as source and destination address, and a piece of the data being transmitted.

Version	Header Length	Type of Service	Total Length		
Identification			IP Flags	Fragment Offset	
Time to Live		Protocol	Header Checksum		
Source Address					
Destination Address					
IP Options					
Data/Message					

Packet Switching a network configuration where data is divided into small units called packets.

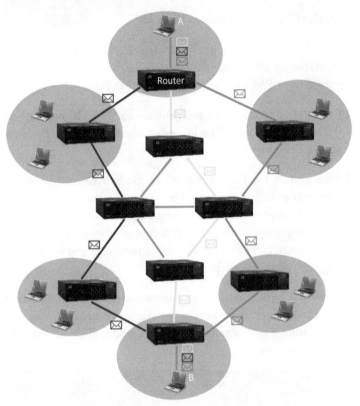

The data or message is divided up into multiple packets, for example, in the diagram above, the message is divided up into 3 packets (illustrated by the coloured envelopes in the diagram). Each packet is sent along a different route (illustrated by the coloured lines).

After reaching the destination through various different routes on the network, the packets are arranged in the original order according to the packet sequence number, there by reconstructing the message.

Page in DRAM memory, is the number of bits that can be accessed from one row address. The size of a page is determined by the number of column addresses. For example, a device with 10 column address pins has a page depth of 1024 bits.

PAL is short for Phase Alternating Line and is a video format used in most of Western Europe, Australia and China as well as in various African, South American and Middle Eastern countries. PAL has a 4:3 image format, 625 lines per frame, a field frequency of 50Hz and 4 MHz video bandwidth with a total 8 MHz of video channel width. PAL has a 25-frame per second update rate and uses YUV colour space.

PAN is short for Personal Area Network and allows devices such as cellphones, headphones, tablets, mice, and keyboards to connect wirelessly within the one's personal space often using bluetooth.

PanelLink was developed by Silicon Images Inc. to provide an all digital link between a graphics card and an LCD monitor, PanelLink uses Transition Minimised Differential Signalling (TMDS) signalling technology, allowing a distance of up to 10m between the graphics card and the LCD panel.

Parallel Port is an I/O channel for a parallel device, like a printer, which sends and receives data eight bits at a time over 8 separate wires. Maximum throughput is around 500 Kbit/s.

Parallelogram Distortion is a type of geometric distortion, where lines are parallel but not perpendicular.

Parity is a data encoding scheme that devices use to check the validity of transmitted characters. This scheme adds an extra bit to each character, set by the transmitting computer based on the type of parity the computers agree to use (odd or even). For example, if the computers use even parity, the transmitting computer sets or clears the parity bit so that there are an even number of bits set in each character it transmits. The receiving computer checks each character and flags a parity error if any character has an odd number of bits set.

Parity Memory is a common method for ensuring the integrity of data stored in memory in which an additional data bit is generated and added to each data byte. Parity is able to detect only single bit errors reliably but cannot perform any correction. If more than one bit has been corrupted, the parity check may not detect a problem. The most commonly used forms of parity are even parity, odd parity, and checksums.

Particle Animation is rendering a 3D scene as millions of discrete particles rather than smooth, texture-mapped surfaces. Much more flexible but computer intensive.

Partition is a logical division of the storage area of a hard disk drive that can be managed separately.

Partition Table is the table located in the boot sector of a hard disk drive that lists all partitions on the disk.

Passive Matrix is a common LCD technology used in laptops. Passive matrix displays are not quite as sharp and do not have as broad a viewing angle as active matrix (TFT) displays.

Patch Cable is a short UTP cable usually used to connect patch panels to a network switch.

Patch Panel is a mountable panel that contains ports used to connect and manage LAN cables in a central point. From the front of the panel, the ports are usually 'patched in' to a core switch using a patch cable.

On the back of the panel, the Cat5 cables are terminated with a punch down or krone tool. These terminated cables run from another device such as a PC, printer, phone, or server, usually in another room or part of the building.

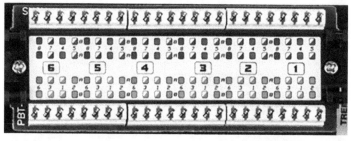

PCB is short for Printed Circuit Board and is a board printed with layers of circuits.

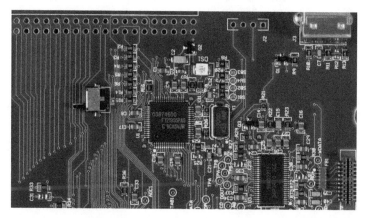

PCI stands for Peripheral Component Interface and is the 32-bit bus architecture widely used in Pentium-based PCs. A PCI bus provides a high bandwidth data channel between system board components such as the CPU and devices such as hard disks and video adapters.

PCI Express short for Peripheral Component Interconnect Express and is a high speed industry-standard bus used for adding additional internal components such as graphics cards, and certain SSD drives to a computer. PCIe x16: has 16 lanes and is mainly used for high end graphics cards. PCIe x1: has 1 lane PCIe x4: has 4 lanes.

PCL short for Printer Control Language and is a protocol designed by Hewlett- Packard to allow PCs to communicate with its laser printers. PCL has become a de facto standard for laser and ink jet printers and is supported by virtually all printer manufacturers. "HP compatible

PCM short for Pulse Coded Modulation and is a technique for converting an analogue signal with an infinite number of possible values into discrete binary digital words that have a finite number of values. The waveform is sampled, then the sample is quantised into PCM codes. PCM is a digitisation technique used by the CCITT V.90 standard , not a universally accepted standard in its own right.

PCMCIA stands for Personal Computer Memory Card International Association and is a consortium of computer manufacturers that devised the standard for the credit card-size adapter cards used in many old notebook computers.

PCMCIA defines three card types:

- Type I cards can be up to 3.3mm thick and are generally used for RAM and ROM expansion cards
- Type II cards can be as thick as 5.5mm and typically house modems and fax modems
- Type III cards are the largest of the lot (up to 10.5mm thick) and are mostly used for solid state disks or miniature hard disks. PCMCIA cards are also known as PC Cards.

PCS stands for Personal Communications Services and is the collective term for US mobile telephone services in the 1900MHz frequency band.

PCX is a popular bitmapped graphics file format originally developed by ZSOFT for its PC Paintbrush program. PCX handles monochrome, 2-bit, 4-bit, 8-bit and 24-bit colour and uses Run Length Encoding (RLE) to achieve compression ratios of approximately 1.1:1 to 1.5:1.

PDA stands for Personal Digital Assistant and is a handheld device that combines computing, telephone/fax, and networking features. A typical PDA can function as a cellular phone, fax sender, and personal organiser. Some PDAs are hand-held PC with tiny keyboards. Another class of device uses a touch-screen and stylus for data entry.

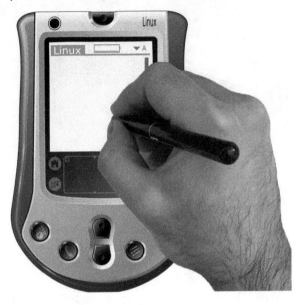

PDC stands for Personal Digital Cellular and is a Japanese standard for digital mobile telephony in the 800MHz and 1500MHz bands.

PDF stands for Portable Document Format and is a file format containing embedded fonts and graphics that is readable on various different operating systems and platforms.

PDL stands for Page Description Language and is a language for describing the layout and contents of a printed page used with laser printers. The best- known PDLs are Adobe PostScript and Hewlett-Packard PCL (Printer Control Language). Both PostScript and modern versions of PC

PDP stands for Plasma Display Panel and is a display technology that works on the principle that passing a high voltage through a low- pressure gas creates light.

Peer-to-Peer is a network architecture in which each workstation has equivalent capabilities and responsibilities. Contrast Client-Server.

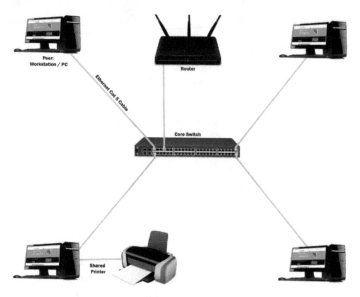

Performance is a measure of the speed of the drive during normal operation. Factors affecting performance are seek times, transfer rate, and command overhead.

Peripheral is a device connected to a computer that is external to the CPU. Examples include printers, cameras, mice, keyboards, scanners. As well as internal components such as hard disk drives and dvd drives.

Perspective Correction is the adjustment of texture maps on objects, viewed at an angle (typically large, flat objects) in order to retain the appearance of perspective.

PGA stands for Pin Grid Array and is a square chip package of either ceramic or plastic, with a high density of pins (typically 200 pins can fit in 1.5in square). In an SPGA (Staggered PGA), the pins are staggered and do not line up in perfect rows and columns.

Phantom Power is DC power transmitted through XLR cables to operate condenser microphones and other devices that contain active electronic circuitry. Usually 48-volt.

Pharming pronounced 'farming', this social engineering technique is designed to redirect a legitimate website's traffic to a duplicate fake site by either using the infected computer's hosts file, the victim's internet router, or a compromised DNS server.

Phishing pronounced 'fishing', this social engineering technique is designed to trick a user into handing over confidential information. Many phishing scams come via an email or phone call that appear to originate from a legitimate source, such as a bank, the police, IRS (HMRC), or a well known company.

Phosphor is a luminescent substance used to coat the inside of the cathode-ray tube display, that is illuminated by the electron gun in the pattern of graphical images as the display is scanned.

Phosphor Triad is one red, one green and one blue phosphor that composes a pixel.

Photolithography is the process of reproducing the chip's circuitry pattern onto the wafer surface by using ultraviolet light and stencils or masks to transfer the image photomechanically.

Photoresist is a material which becomes soluble when exposed to ultraviolet light. Used to help define circuit patterns during chip fabrication where it prevents etching or plating of the area it covers; also called resist.

PHP is short for Hypertext Preprocessor and is a widely-used open source scripting language used in web development. PHP code is processed on the web server by a PHP interpreter.

Physical Format is the actual physical layout of cylinders, tracks, and sectors on a disk drive.

Physical Modelling Synthesis is a revolutionary method for generating sound. This technique emulates the impulse patterns of real-world instruments using a software model.

PIC stands for Programmable Interrupt Controller and is a chip or device that prioritises interrupt requests generated by keyboards, serial ports, and other devices and passes them on to the CPU in order of highest priority. See also IRQ.

Picolitre pl: a million millionth of a litre.

Piezo-Electric is the property of certain crystals that causes them to oscillate when subjected to electrical pressure (voltage).

Pigment Inks consist of tiny chunks of solid pigment suspended in a liquid solution. According to their proponents, pigment inks offer richer, deeper colours and have less tendency to run, bleed or f

Pincushion Distortion is the opposite of barrel distortion. The vertical lines in a rectangular image curve inwards, with an increase in the distortion towards the edges of the image.

PIO stands for Programmed Input Output Mode and is a method of transferring data to and from a storage device (hard disk or CD device) controller to memory via the computer's I/O ports, where the CPU plays a pivotal role in managing the throughput. For optimal performance a controller should support the drive's highest PIO mode (usually PIO mode 4).

Pipeline in DRAMs and SRAMs, is a method of increasing the performance using multistage circuitry to stack or save data while new data is being accessed. The depth of a pipeline varies from product to product. For example, in an EDO DRAM, one bit of data appears on the output while the next bit is being accessed. In some SRAMs, pipelines may contain bits of data or more.

Pipeline Burst Cache is a type of synchronous cache that uses two techniques to minimise processor wait states – a burst mode that pre- fetches memory contents before they are requested, and pipelining so that one memory value can be accessed in the cache at the same time that another memory value is accessed in DRAM.

Pipeline Processing is a category of techniques that provide simultaneous, or parallel, processing within a CPU. It refers to overlapping operations by moving data or instructions into a conceptual pipe with all stages of the pipe processing simultaneously. For example, while one instruction is being executed, the computer is decoding the next instruction.

Pixel is an abbreviation for picture element. In a raster grid, the pixel is the smallest unit that can be addressed and given a colour or intensity. The pixel is represented by some number of bits (usually 8, 16 or 24) in the frame buffer, and is illuminated by a collection of phosphor dots in the CRT that are struck by the beams of the electron

Pixel Clock Speed is the frequency or speed at which individual pixels (picture elements) in an image are written to the screen. The higher the pixel clock speed, the less likely there will be flicker.

Pixelization is the graininess of an image that results when an image is enlarged. Also referred to as Pixelated.

Plated Media are the disks that are covered with a hard metal alloy instead of an iron-oxide compound. Plated disks can store more data than their oxide-coated counter-parts.

Platform is a computer system consisting of hardware and an operating system that a computer program can run on. The term often refers to a device's operating system such as Windows running on a PC, Android or iOS running on a smart phone, or MacOS running on a Mac.

Platter is a disk made of metal (or other rigid material) that is mounted inside a fixed disk drive. Most drives use more than one platter mounted on a single spindle (shaft) to provide more data storage surfaces in a smaller area.

PM stands for Phase Modulation and is a data transmission technique that encodes a data signal into a carrier by varying (or modulating) the phase of the carrier. The phase is the position of a single point on the wave.

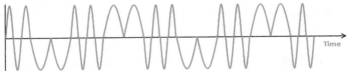

PMOS stands for P-channel Metal Oxide Semiconductor and pertains to MOS devices constructed on an N-type silicon substrate in which holes flow between source and drain contacts.

PnP stands for Plug and Play and is a Microsoft/Intel specification that allows for self-configuration of computer peripherals. Adding a PnP compliant device to a PnP enabled PC requires little more than making the physical connection. The operating system, in conjunction with PnP logic present in the BIOS and in the device itself, handles the IRQ settings, I/O addresses, and other technical aspects of the installation to ensure that the device does not conflict with other installed devices.

PoE stands for Power over Ethernet (PoE) is a standard for providing DC electrical power along with data over twisted pair ethernet cabling. There are two modes:

Mode A also known as endspan, transmits both data and power on the orange and green pairs. This method is best when both power and data originate from the same power sourcing equipment.

Mode B also known as midspan, transmits power over the blue and brown pairs and data on the orange and green pairs.

Mode A			Mode B		
Pin No.	**Marking**	**Colour**	**Pin No.**	**Marking**	**Colour**
1	Tx+ DC+		1	Tx+	
2	Tx − DC+		2	Tx −	
3	Rx+ DC-		3	Rx+	
4			4	PoE +	
5			5	PoE +	
6	Rx − DC-		6	Rx −	
7			7	PoE -	
8			8	PoE -	

PoE injectors that inject power into a standard Ethernet ports often use Mode B to power devices. The power supply is usually between 44 − 57v, although 48v is used for most devices. PoE can be used to power wireless access points, VoIP phones, and IP cameras. PoE (802.3af) is the original PoE standard and provides 15.4W of power the device at 100m distance from the switch. PoE+(802.3at) provides 30W of power to the device at 100m distance from the switch. PoE++(802.3bt) doubles the PoE+ power to the device by providing 60W or 90W of power at 100m distance from the switch.

Polygon is any closed shape with four or more sides. In 3D, complex objects like teapots are decomposed, or "tessellated", into many primitive polygons to allow regular processing of the data, and hardware acceleration of that processing.

Polygon-Based Modelling is representing 3D objects as a set or mesh of polygons.

Polyphony is the number of voices a synthesiser can play at any one time.

Polysilicon is the conductive material used as an interconnect layer on a chip.

POP3 stands for Post Office Protocol, or sometimes Point of Presence, and is a mail protocol that was used to retrieve email from a mail server.

POSIX stands for Portable Operating System Interface for UNIX and is a set of IEEE and ISO standards that define an interface between programs and operating systems. By designing their programs to conform to POSIX, developers have some assurance that their software can be easily ported to POSIX-compliant operating systems. This includes most varieties of UNIX.

POST stands for Power-On Self-Test and is a set of diagnostic routines that execute when a computer is first powered on.

PostScript is a page description language developed by Adobe. Generally used by laser printers, PostScript is becoming increasingly common in high-end inkjets too.

POTS stands for Plain Old Telephone Service and is the basic analogue telephone service with no added features, such as call waiting or call forwarding.

PPP stands for Point to Point Protocol and is a protocol that operates at layer 2 allowing data communication between two network entities or points. PPP is used by Internet service providers (ISPs) to enable connections to the Internet.

PPPoA is short for Point-to-Point Protocol over ATM and is a protocol that operates at layer 2 commonly used to connect domestic broadband modems to an ISP via telephone line.

PPPoE is short for Point-to-Point Protocol over Ethernet and is a network protocol for encapsulating Point-to-Point Protocol frames inside Ethernet frames.

Prefetch Unit is the unit that decides when to order data and instructions from the Instruction Cache, or the computer's main memory based on commands or the task being executed. When the instructions come in, the prefetch unit makes sure all the instructions are lined up correctly to send off to the decode unit.

Pretexting is a social engineering technique that uses a fabricated scenario designed to gain a user's trust and trick them into handing over personal information. This scam is usually a phone call that appears to come from an authority such as the police or tax office, but could also impersonate a co-worker, an insurance company, some fake organisation running bogus special offers, or some external IT support company.

Primitives are the smallest units in the 3D graphics usually points, lines, and polygons representing basic geometric shapes, such as spheres, cubes, and cylinders. Some 3D hardware and software schemes also employ curves, known as "splines".

Printer is a peripheral device used to make hard copy representations of graphics, photos or text on paper.

Printer Dot is the individual pixel in a halftone image. The size of a printer dot is variable, ranging from zero (all white) to the size of the halftone screen (all black).

PRML stands for Partial Response Maximum Likelihood and is a technique used to differentiate a valid signal from noise which achieves improved accuracy by looking at entire waveforms rather than just peaks in isolation, using digital signal processing (DSP) to reconstruct recorded data. On magnetic disks PRML uses RLL encoding to provide a ratio of user data to recorded data of 8:9.

Process Colours are the four primary ink colours Cyan, Magenta, Yellow and Black (CMYK) used in colour printing.

Protected Mode is a memory-addressing system that keeps the executing programs within their memory boundaries.

Protocol is a formal set of rules and descriptions that allow two computers to exchange information.

PS/2 is an IBM personal computer series introduced in 1987, superseding the original PC line.

PSK stands for Phase Shift Keying is a data transmission technique that blends a data signal into a carrier by varying (modulating) the phase of the carrier by a certain number of degrees for each succeeding signal.

PSTN is short for Public Switched Telephone Network and refers to the international telephone system based on copper wires carrying analogue voice data.

PSU is short for Power Supply Unit and is the component inside the computer that supplies power to the motherboard and internal drives.

Psychoacoustics is the study of how the human brain perceives sound. Findings relating to which sounds are and are not heard by the human ear have been used in the formulation of various audio compression techniques, including MP3.

Pulse Dialling is a method of dialling the telephone where the modem sends pulses (which you hear through the handset as clicks) to represent the telephone numbers (one pulse for a one, two pulses for a two, etc.). Pulse dialling is normally associated with rotary-dial phones. See also Tone Dialling.

PVR stands for Personal Video Recorder and is a generic term for the modern-day replacement of the VCR. Using hardware-based MPEG-2 compression like that used by DVDs, PVRs encode video data and store the data on a hard disk drive. PVRs have all of the functionality of VCRs, (recording, playback, fast forwarding, rewinding, pausing) plus the ability to instantly jump to any part of the program without having to rewind or fast forward the data stream. Also referred to a Digital Video Recorder.

Q

QAM is short for Quadrature Amplitude Modulation and is modulation technique used by high speed modems combining two amplitude-modulated (AM) signals into a single channel, thereby doubling the effective bandwidth.

Quantisation is the process of representing a voltage with a discrete binary digital number. Approximating an infinite valued signal with a finite number system introduces an error called quantisation error or noise.

Queue is an abstract data structure in which items are stored in order. See FIFO and LIFO. Also an area where processes await their turn to be executed by a CPU.

QuickTime is Apple Computer's multimedia framework for processing video, audio and pictures.

QWERTY is a keyboard layout originally created in the 1870s by Christopher Sholes for manual typewriters. The layout is used for Latin-script alphabets whose name comes from the first letters of the top row of the keyboard.

~ `	! 1	@ 2	# 3	$ 4	% 5	^ 6	& 7	* 8	(9	) 0	_ -	+ =	← Backspace
Tab	Q	W	E	R	T	Y	U	I	O	P	{ [	}]	| \
Caps Lock	A	S	D	F	G	H	J	K	L	: ;	" '	Enter ↵	
Shift	Z	X	C	V	B	N	M	< ,	> .	? /	Shift		
Ctrl	Win Key	Alt					Alt	Win Key	Menu	Ctrl			

The layout wasn't actually designed to slow down the typist but rather make it more efficient when touch typing.

R

RADIUS stands for Remote Authentication Dial-In User Service protocol and is a client/server security protocol that allows network managers to centralise user authentication on a single server. This means users can use one set of network credentials to access various network resources such as a WiFi network, NAS drive share and so on.

RADSL stands for Rate Adaptive Digital Subscriber Line and is an implementation of ADSL that automatically adjusts the connection speed on start up to adjust for the quality of the telephone line, thereby allowing the service to function over longer distances than does ordinary ADSL.

RAID stands for Redundant Array of Independent Disks and is a data storage virtualization technology that combines multiple hard disk drives into a storage array for the purposes of data redundancy, performance, or both.

RAID 0 data is striped across two or more disks to increase performance. This setup provides no fault tolerance, if one drive fails all the data is lost. A file is split into blocks, half the blocks go on disk 1, the other half go on disk 2.

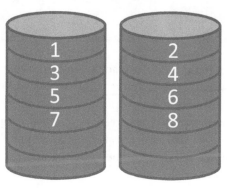

RAID 1 usually consists of two drives. Data is written to one drive then mirrored (copied) to the second drive. This setup provides fault tolerance, if one drive fails the data is recoverable from the second drive.

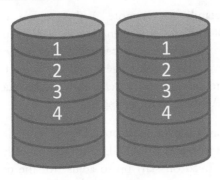

RAID 5 usually uses three or more drives. The data is striped across the drives with parity check. This provides both performance and fault tolerance. If a drive fails, the data can be reconstructed using the parity data.

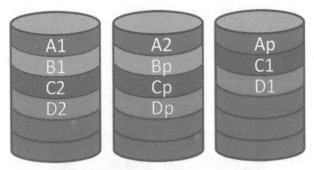

Rainbow Effect is an artefact unique to single-chip DLP projectors which appears as a rainbow or multi-colour shimmer briefly noticeable by some people when they change focus from one part of the projector screen to another. It appears as a secondary image that appears at the viewer's peripheral vision and is typically noticeable when shifting focus from a high contrast area or bright object.

RAM stands for Random Access Memory and is the primary storage location used to store working data and program code in a computer system. Each memory location can be accessed directly. RAM is volatile, meaning the data is lost when the power is cut.

RAM Disk is a virtual drive created by setting aside a section of RAM and accessed as if it were a disk drive. Access to a RAM disk is very fast but data is lost when the system is reset or turned off.

RAMDAC converts the data in the frame buffer into the RGB signal required by the monitor.

Random Access is the ability to access any particular block by going directly to it. Memory and disk devices support random access; by contrast, tape storage devices do not.

Ransomware is a malicious program designed to encrypt and lock a computer system until a fee is paid effectively holding the system to ransom. Ransomware attacks are usually carried out using a trojan worm that a user is tricked into opening. These trojans can arrive through email or from a phishing scam.

RAS stands for Row Address Select (or Strobe) and is a control pin on DRAM memory used to latch and activate a row address. The row selected is determined by the data present at the address pins when RAS becomes active.

RAS Line is a physical track on motherboard used to select which sides of which SIMMs will be involved in a data transfer. A given chipset supports only a certain number of RAS lines, thereby dictating how many SIMMs can be accommodated. A pair of SIMMs uses one RAS line; a pair of DIMMs uses two.

Raster is a rectangular grid of picture elements representing graphical data for display. Raster operations (ROPs) can be performed on some portion or all of the raster.

Raster Image is an image defined as a set of dots/pixels in a column- and-row format. Rasterisation is the process of determining values for the dots/pixels in a rendered image. See also Bitmap.

Rasterization is the conversion of a polygon 3D scene, stored in a frame buffer, into an image complete with textures, depth cues and lighting.

RCA stands for Radio Corporation of America and refers to the standard single ended analogue cables used to connect audio and video devices together. Typically red/white inputs are for the left/right channels of sound and yellow is for video.

Read After Write is a mode of operation that has the computer read back each sector immediately after it is written on the disk, checking that the data read back is the same as recorded. This slows disk operations, but raises reliability.

Read Channel is a circuit on a hard disk drive that converts the digital data into magnetic flux changes for recording to the disk's magnetic surface, and vice versa.

Read Verify is a disk mode where the disk reads in data to the controller, but the controller only checks for errors and does not pass the data on to the system.

Recovery Console is a command line tool included in Windows that is sometimes used to repair the system where you can run commands such as diskpart, chkdsk and fixboot and so on.

Read/Write Head is a device which uses induction to write a data pattern onto magnetic media, and uses inductance or magneto-resistance to read the data back.

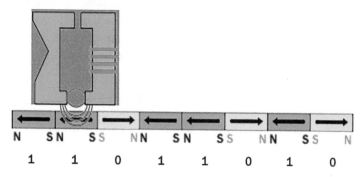

Heads come in many different shapes and forms, and are used for both contact and non- contact type recording. Here below is an example of a read/write head in a hard disk drive.

RealAudio is an audio compression scheme used on the Internet to provide streamed audio.

Real-time refers to an operating mode under which data is received and processed and the results returned so quickly as to seem instantaneous.

Rear Projection the projector is placed behind a translucent screen. See also Front Projection.

Reed-Solomon is an error-correction encoding system that cycles data multiple times through a mathematical transformation in order to increase the effectiveness of the error correction, especially for burst errors (ie errors that occur closely together such as a physical defect).

Reflections are sounds that originate from a sound source and bounce off walls, floors, ceilings and other obstructions before reaching the listener.

Refresh is the process used to restore the charge in DRAM memory cells at specified intervals. The required refresh interval is a function of the memory cell design and the semiconductor technology used to manufacture the memory device. There are several refresh schemes that may be used.

Refresh Rate is expressed in Hertz (Hz), and in interlaced mode is the number of fields written to the screen every second. In non-interlaced mode it is the number of frames written to the screen every second. Higher frequencies reduce flicker, because they light the pixels more frequently, reducing the dimming that causes flicker. Also called vertical frequency.

Regedit is a tool included in Windows that allows you to edit the system registry. See Registry

Registered Memory is a type of SDRAM memory that uses registers to hold data for one clock cycle before it is moving it on and in so doing increases the reliability of high-speed data access. Registered memory modules are typically used only in server environments and other mission-critical systems. Registered and unbuffered memory cannot be mixed. the design of the processor's memory controller dictating which type is required.

218

Registers are a mini-storage area for data used by the Arithmetic Logic Unit (ALU) to complete the tasks the Control Unit has requested. The data can come from the data cache, main memory or the control unit and are all stored at special locations within the Registers. This makes retrieval for the ALU quick and efficient.

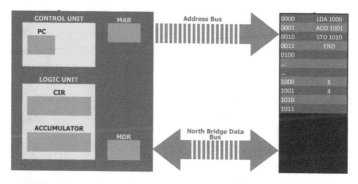

Registry is a hierarchical database used to store configuration information in Windows. See Regedit

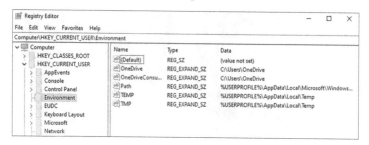

Reliable Connection is a connection between two modems where they communicate using an error control protocol (such as LAPM or MNP).

Removable Disk is any disk drive where the disk itself can be removed. Their advantage is that multiple disks can be used to increase the amount of stored material, and that once removed, the disk can be stored away to prevent unauthorised use.

Removable Storage is a type of storage which allows the actual storage media to be removed from a drive and replace it with other media. It is used for the transportation of data between computers and for data backup.

Rendering is the drawing of an effect or scene as it appears.

Request To Send or simply **RTS** is an RS-232C signal that requests the modem to send data. It initiates any data transmission between the computer (or terminal) and the modem. It is answered by a Clear To Send (CTS) signal.

Resistor is an electronic component that resists the flow of current in an electronic circuit.

Resolution is the number of pixels per unit of area, usually measured in pixels or dots per inch. The finer the grid defining an area, the more pixels it contains and the higher its resolution. The higher the resolution the greater its detail.

Response Time when referring to LCD monitors is the time it takes for the liquid crystal inside a screen panel to respond to applied current. Also the time it takes for a component to respond to a command.

Reverb or Reverberation is the sum of all sound reflections or echoes in a given environment.

RF stands for Radio Frequency and is the range of electromagnetic frequencies above the audio range and below visible light. All broadcast transmission, from AM radio to satellites, falls into this range, which is between 30KHz and 300GHz.

RGB short for Red-Green-Blue, an additive colour model for displaying images in computer graphics by describing the amount of each of the three primary colours: Red, Green and Blue. Three bytes are required for "true colour" (three numbers between 0 and 255), giving a theoretical maximum of 16.7 million colours. Here below we can see the colour green shown in Photoshop's colour picker.

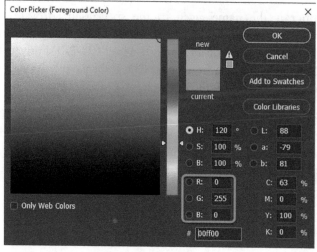

Computer monitors use an RGB signal.

RIAA stands for Recording Industry Association of America: The association formed by the recording companies in the United States to promote the recording industry and to defend its legal rights. The RIAA equalisation curve is a compensation method applied to a signal from a record deck pick-up. Phono pre-amps have RIAA circuitry built-in.

RIFF stands for Resource Interchange File Format and is a platform-independent multimedia specification (published by Microsoft and others in 1990) that allows audio, image, animation, and other multimedia elements to be stored in a common format. See also Media Control Interface (MCI).

RIMM stands for Rambus in-line memory module, a memory module similar to DIMMs.

Ripper is the name given to the specialised software that extracts raw audio data from a music CD. The ability to extract audio digitally relies on a feature of newer CD-ROM drives that allows the digital data from audio CDs to be passed through the computer's bus (IDE, SCSI) just like CD-ROM data.

RISC stands for Reduced Instruction Set Computer. RISC processors use simple instructions that are executed within one clock cycle. RISC instructions operate only on processor registers and are fast.

```
LDA 1000
ADD 1001
STO 1010
```

This processor architecture is used in cellular smartphones and some computer tables.

RJ11 is a common jack type most often used for connecting analogue phones, modems, and fax machines to a phone line. Contains 6 wires but only the middle 2 are normally used for a single device.

RJ45 stands for Registered Jack (RJ) number 45 and is a standardized network interface for connecting data devices such as computers, ethernet switches and routers. Twisted pair Ethernet cables are terminated with a standard RJ45 connector.

Each of the wires is inserted into an RJ45 plug using either the T-568A spec, or more commonly the T-586B spec, as shown below:

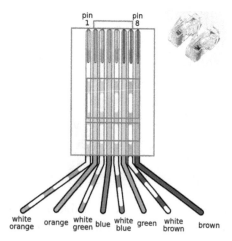

Twisted pair cabling is comprised of two independently insulated wires twisted around each other in varying degrees of twist. The orange pair is twisted more tightly than the brown pair. This helps to counteract noise and interference. These cables come in unshielded (UTP) and shielded (STP) versions. Devices are connected individually to a switch, so if one connection fails, the rest of the network can continue to operate.

RLE stands for Run Length Encoding and is Microsoft's video compression algorithm for base level multimedia PCs. Compresses 8-bit sequences only. Playback is also in 8 bit and isn't scalable for higher power PCs.

RLL short for Run Length Limited and is a method used on some hard disks to encode data into magnetic pulses. RLL requires more processing, but stores almost 50 percent more data per disk than the older MFM (modified frequency modulation) method. The run length is the maximum number of consecutive 0s before a 1 bit is recorded.

Roland GS is Roland General Synthesiser and General MIDI two overlapping specifications for defining the standard sets of MIDI sounds that are associated with specific commands.

ROM stands for Read Only Memory and is a non-volatile memory or storage containing data that cannot be changed. Read Only Memory is useful for storing a program that very rarely change. An example is the BIOS program needed to start a PC, sometimes known as firmware.

Rootkit is a program designed to enable unauthorised, remote administrator access to a computer by opening a backdoor. Rootkits don't replicate themselves like worms and viruses do and are usually installed through phishing scams, executable files, or software downloaded from a dodgy website. Once installed, an attacker can connect to the infected machine and introduce other malware to steal information. Rootkits usually hide themselves on the infected machine and can be difficult to detect.

Rotation determines how well the image area lines up to the bezel; also called tilt.

Round Robin Scheduling is a process scheduling system where each process is given a fixed amount of execution time (quantum). A process is executed until its time expires. This process is then suspended, and the next process begins its execution...

When all the processes in the queue have been allocated an amount of time, the scheduler returns to the beginning of the process queue and starts again.

Router is a layer 3 network device responsible for forwarding data packets between computer networks based on the network address. For example at home, the device that connects your laptop, tablet, or smartphone to the internet is called a router.

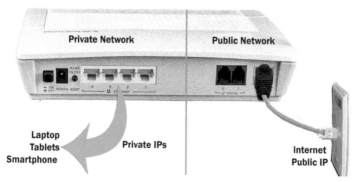

Row is part of the RAM array. A bit is stored where a column and a row intersect.

RPC is short for Remote Procedure Call, a protocol that enables a program to request services from another computer on a network or the internet.

RPM stands for Revolutions Per Minute and is a measure of rotational speed.

RS-232 is a standardised connection system for connecting a device to the serial port of a computer or terminal. This is the recommended standard of the Electronic Industries Association (EIA) for exchanging information between DTE (such as computers) and DCE (such as modems).

RTF short for Rich Text Format: a format commonly used by most word processors that contains the text, formatting, images, and page layout.

S

S/PDIF stands for Sony/Philips Digital Interchange Format and is an interface standard used to connect consumer audio equipment using either coaxial cable with RCA connectors or optical cable with TOSLINK connectors.

Sampling is the process of converting an analogue signal into a digital representation. This is accomplished by measuring the value of the analogue signal at regular intervals called samples. These values are then encoded to provide a digital representation of the analogue signal.

Sampling Rate is the frequency with which samples are taken and converted into digital form. The sampling frequency should be at least twice that of the analogue frequency being digitised. Thus, the sampling rate for hi-fi playback is 44.1kHz, slightly more than double the 20kHz frequency humans can hear.

SAN stands for Storage Area Network and is a high-speed special purpose network containing disk arrays for data storage and provides a shared pool of storage space. Each user connected to a SAN can access that data as if it were a local disk connected directly to the computer.

SAS stands for Serial Attached SCSI, and is a serial interface for connecting high speed hard drives to a computer, replacing old parallel SCSI.

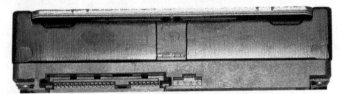

The drive is connected using a SAS drive cable.

SATA stands for **S**erial **A**dvanced **T**echnology **A**ttachment. SATA is an interface that connects mass storage devices such as hard drives, solid-state drives and other types of drive to a computer's motherboard. SATA is based on serial signalling technology, a single cable with a minimum of four wires creating a point-to-point connection between devices.

The drive is connected using a SATA data cable (below left) and a SATA power cable (below right).

Saturated Colours are strong, bright colours (particularly reds and oranges) which do not reproduce well on video; they tend to saturate the screen with colour or bleed around the edges, producing a garish, unclear image.

Saturation is the intensity of a colour or hue. For example, a fully saturated blue would be a pure, bright blue. A less saturated blue, the more pastel the appearance. See also Chroma.

SCA stands for Single Connector Attachment and is the same speed SCSI interface as LVD, but integrates power and I/O information into a single 80-pin connector. Used in high-end servers to allow hard disks to be hot- swapped in a RAID array.

Scalability is the ability to vary the information content of a program by changing the amount of data that is stored, transmitted or displayed. In a video image, this translates into creating larger or smaller windows of video on screens (shrinking effect).

Scaling the process of changing the size of characters or graphics.

Screen Door Effect (SDE) is common with LCD-based projectors and relates to a viewer's awareness of the grid, or spacing between the pixels. The lines which form the grid are, in fact, where the panel's control electronics are preventing light from shining through the panel.

Screen Regulation is a distortion where the size of the image varies according to the brightness of the screen content. A white rectangle will appear larger when surrounding a solid white rectangle than when surrounding a plain black area.

SCSI stands for Small Computer System Interface and is a parallel interface for attaching disk drives, scanners, printers, and other peripherals to a computer. Internal SCSI disk drives were attached to a host controller using a 68 pin ribbon cable.

You could connect up to 15 devices to a host controller creating a SCSI chain. External SCSI devices used a 50 pin cable

SD Card stands for Secure Digital Card and is a memory card commonly used in digital cameras, laptops, tablets, and phones to store data. They come in standard size and micro.

| Standard SD | Micro SD | SD Card Adapter |

SDLC stands Software Development Life cycle and is a methodology used to develop software.

Analysis, design, implementation, testing, deployment.

SDMI stands for Secure Digital Music Initiative and is a secure digital format for distributing music over the Internet. Announced in February 1999, it was backed by the Recording Industry Association of America (RIAA) and Sony, Warner, BMG, EMI and Universal – the top five music production companies..

SDRAM Synchronous DRAM, a type of DRAM that delivers bursts of data at very high speeds synchronised by an external clock signal. See DDR., DRAM.

SDTV stands for Standard definition television, a television broadcast system with resolutions of 720 x 480, or 720 x 576. See HDTV

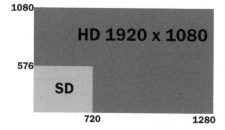

SEC or SECC short for Single Edge Contact Cartridge, and is a processor module first used by Intel's Pentium II CPU. It comprised of a hardware module that contained the CPU itself and an external L2 cache.

The module plugged into a slot (called Slot 1, Slot 2, or Slot A) on the motherboard .

SECAM stands for Sequentiel Coleur A Memoire and is a video standard, used in France and Eastern Europe with image format 4:3, 819 lines per frame, 50 Hz and 6 MHz video bandwidth with a total 8 MHz of video channel width. Like the similar PAL standard, it has a 25-frame per second update rate. The major difference from PAL is that SECAM uses FM-modulated chrominance.

Sector is the minimum segment of track length that can be assigned to store data. Magnetic disks are typically divided into tracks, each which contains a number of sectors. A sector contains a predetermined amount of data, such as 512 bytes.

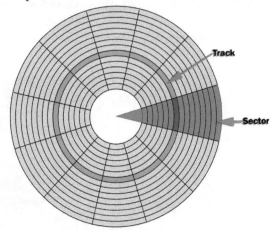

Seek Time is the time taken for the actuator to move the heads to the correct cylinder in order to access data.

Semiconductor is a solid-state substance with conductive properties that can be altered with electricity. Silicon performs as a semiconductor when chemically combined with other elements. A semiconductor is also halfway between a conductor and an insulator. When charged with electricity or light, semiconductors change their state from non conductive to conductive or vice versa. The most significant product built from a semiconductor is the transistor.

Sequencer is software for recording and editing MIDI files.

Serial Port is a connector that facilitate communication between a computer and a serial devices such as a modems, plotter, or mouse, and other equipment. On a PC, this socket is a DB-9 male connector.

It is a full-duplex device, using separate lines for transmitting and receiving data at the same time. Maximum throughput is 115.2 Kbit/s. Also called a COM or communications port.

Server is a computer program usually running on a large computer that delivers a service to other devices on a network. There are various types of server. A web server hosts websites and serves web pages. A file server stores and serves files. A mail server stores email accounts and messages.

Servo Motor is a motor used for precise control of angular and linear movements often used in robotics.

Settle Time is the interval between the arrival of the read/write head at a specific track, and the lessening of the residual movement to a level sufficient for reliable reading or writing.

Setup is the conversion of a set of instructions concerning the size, shape and position of polygons into a 3D scene ready for rasterization.

SGRAM stands for Synchronous Graphics RAM and is a single ported DRAM designed for high-speed, serial data, and usually used on graphics boards.

Shader is an algorithm which mathematically describes how an individual material is rendered to an object and how light interacts with its overall appearance.

Shading is the process of creating pixel colours. Gouraud is a constant increment of colour from one pixel to the next, while Phong is much more complex and higher quality. Flat shading means no smooth blending of colours, each polygon being a single colour.

Shadow Mask is the perforated metal sheet that rests between the electron gun and a screen's phosphor coating to ensure that the three electron beams only strike the correct phosphor dots. A "shadow mask display" is a monitor which conforms to the conventional three- electron gun, shadow mask design.

Shannon's Law defines the relationship between the maximum throughput in any given channel to the presence of noise.

Shock Rating is a rating (expressed in Gs) of how much shock a disk drive can sustain without damage. Operating and non-operating shock levels are usually specified separately.

Shouldering is a social engineering technique used to harvest passwords, PIN numbers and other sensitive data by discretely looking over someone's shoulder while they enter the information.

SIF standard Interchange Format and is a format for exchanging video images of 240 lines with 352 pixels each for NTSC, and 288 lines by 352 pixels for PAL and SECAM. At the nominal field rates of 60 and 50 fields/s, the two formats have the same data rate.

Sign Bit is usually the left most bit of a binary number used to indicate a positive(0) or negative (1) number.

Silicon Dioxide is grown on a wafer during chip fabrication to serve as an insulating layer.

Silicon Ingot is a large, cylindrical, single crystal made from purified silicon. The cylinder is sliced into thin wafers which are used for making computer chips.

Silicon Wafer is a slice of pure silicon used to fabricate integrated circuits such as microprocessors. The individual microcircuits are cut from the wafer using a process called wafer dicing. These microcircuits are then packaged as an integrated circuit.

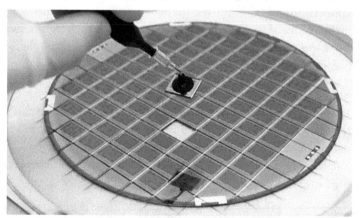

SIM stands for subscriber identity module and is an integrated circuit mounted on a small plastic card used to identify and authenticate subscribers on mobile devices.

SIMM stands for Single In-Line Memory Module and typically come with a 32 data bit with a 72-pin connector that had to be installed in pairs to work properly. They were eventually replaced by the DIMMs.

Single Mode uses only one light ray (or mode) through a 9 micron cable and can transmit up to 100km.

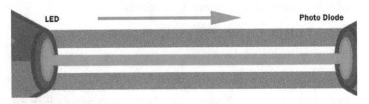

Sledgehammer is the codename for AMD's x86-64 design for extending the iA-32 architecture to support 64-bit code and memory addressing.

SLIP stands for Serial Line Internet Protocol and is a protocol that allows a computer to connect to the Internet through a connection and enjoy most of the benefits of a direct connection, including the ability to run graphical front ends such as Internet Browsers. SLIP is also used to run TCP/IP over phone lines. See also PPP.

Slot 1 is Intel's proprietary CPU interface form factor for Pentium II CPUs. Slot 1 replaces the Socket 7 and Socket 8 form factors used by previous Pentium processors. It is a 242-contact daughterboard slot that accepts a microprocessor packaged as a Single Edge Contact (SEC) cartridge. Communication between the Level 2 cache and CPU is at half the CPU's clock speed.

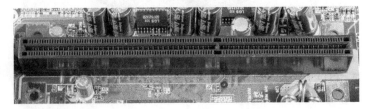

Slot 2 is an enhanced Slot 1, which uses a somewhat wider 330-way connector SEC cartridge that holds up to four processors. The biggest difference from Slot 1 is that the Level 2 runs at full processor speed.

Slot A is AMD's proprietary 242-way connector SEC cartridge used by their original Athlon processor. Physically identical to Slot 1 but electrically incompatible.

Slotted Mask is a variation on the aperture grill phosphor triad approach which uses the slot-mask design used on many non-Trinitron TV sets.

SmartMedia is an ultra-compact flash memory card format developed by Toshiba. Similar to an SD card, but slightly bigger and as thin as a credit card. SmartMedia cards were popular in early digital cameras around 2001 and could hold up to 128MB but were superseded by XD and SD cards.

SMDS stands for Switched Multimegabit Data Service and is a high-speed, switched data communications service offered by telephone companies for interconnecting separate local area networks (LANs) into a single wide area network (WAN). Prior to SMDS's arrival in 1995, the only way to connect LANs was through a dedicated private line. SMDS is becoming an increasingly attractive alternative because it is more flexible and usually more economical.

SMP stands for Symmetric Multiprocessing and is a computer architecture that provides fast performance by making multiple CPUs available to complete individual processes simultaneously (multiprocessing). Unlike asymmetrical processing, any idle processor can be assigned any task, and additional CPUs can be added to improve performance and handle increased loads.

SMPTE Timecode is an 80-bit standardised edit time code adopted by SMPTE, the Society of Motion Picture and Television Engineers. See also Time Code, for measuring video duration. Each frame is identified in the form hours:minutes:seconds:frames.

SMTP stands for Simple Mail Transport Protocol and is the protocol used to send e-mail on the internet.

SNA stands for Systems Network Architecture and is a mainframe network topology introduced by IBM in 1974. Originally designed as a centralised architecture with a host computer controlling many terminals, SNA has evolved over the years so that it now also supports peer-to-peer networks of workstations. SNA incorporates data protocols, network interface cards and just about every facet of communication.

SNR short for Signal-to-Noise Ratio and is a measure of link performance arrived at by dividing signal power by noise power. Typically measured in decibels. The higher the ratio, the clearer the connection.

Socket 370 is Intel's proprietary CPU interface form factor first introduced for its Celeron line of CPUs and subsequently adopted for later versions of the Pentium III family.

Socket 423 is Intel's proprietary CPU interface form factor used by its early Pentium 4 processors.

Socket 478 is Intel's proprietary CPU interface form factor which replaced Socket 423 with the advent of the 0.13-micron Pentium 4 Northwood core.

Socket 7 is the CPU interface form factor for fifth-generation Pentium-class CPU chips from Intel, Cyrix, and AMD.

Socket 754 is AMD's 754-pin CPU interface form factor introduced with its 64-bit Athlon 64 processor in the autumn of 2003.

Socket 8 is Intel's proprietary CPU interface form factor used exclusively by their sixth-generation Pentium Pro CPU chip. Socket 8 is a 387-pin ZIF socket with connections for the CPU and one or two SRAM dies for the Level 2 cache.

Socket A is AMD's 462-pin CPU interface form factor which replaced Slot A at the time of the introduction of the Thunderbird and Spitfire cores used by AMD's Athlon and Duron desktop processor ranges respectively.

Soft Error is an error in data or a signal. It can be corrected using ECC. Usually caused by power fluctuations or noise spikes.

Soft-Sectored disks mark the beginning of each sector of data within a track by a magnetic pattern.

SOHO stands for Small Office/Home Office and refers to a small business or business-at-home user with 1-10 workers.

SOI stands for Silicon-On-Insulator and is a silicon wafer with a thin layer of oxide – into which integrated circuits are built – buried in it. SOI substrates achieve superior isolation between adjacent devices in CMOS devices.

SOJ stands for Small Outline J-Lead package and is a plastic surface mount package designed for memory chips with pins that look like the letter J.

Solid State Drive or SSD, is a mass storage device used to store data on a computer system using flash memory.

Sound Blaster is a family of sound cards developed by Creative Labs.

Sound Card also known as an audio card, is an internal expansion card that facilitates the input and output of audio signals to and from a computer, providing the audio for multimedia applications such as music, editing video or audio, presentations, games and video projection through a speaker or sound system.

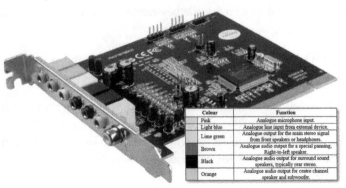

Colour	Function
Pink	Analogue microphone input.
Light blue	Analogue line input from external device.
Lime green	Analogue output for the main stereo signal from front speakers or headphones.
Brown	Analogue audio output for a special panning, Right-to-left speaker.
Black	Analogue audio output for surround sound speakers, typically rear stereo.
Orange	Analogue audio output for centre channel speaker and subwoofer.

South Bridge connects the CPU to the slower devices such as USB ports, hard drives, external drives, printers wifi/network cards, and other peripherals.

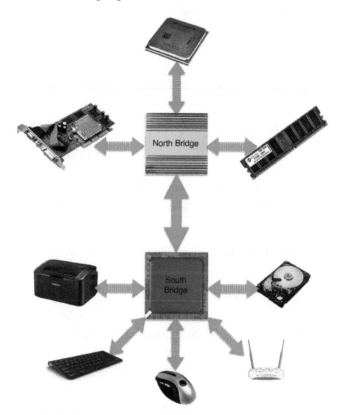

SPDIF see S/PDIF

Specular Highlights are lighting characteristic that determines how light should reflect off an object. Specular highlights are typically white and can move around an object based on camera position.

Spindle is a disk drive's centre shaft on which the disk platters are mounted.

Spindle Speed is the velocity at which the disk media spins within a hard disk, measured in rpm (revolutions per minute). By the late 1990s EIDE hard disks generally features a 5,400rpm or 7,200 mechanism, while SCSI drives were usually either 7,200rpm or 10,000rpm.

Spline is a 3D bezier curve used in modelling.

Spline-Based Modelling is representing 3-D objects as surfaces made up of mathematically derived curves (splines).

Spotify is an audio streaming service where you can stream music and other content free. Spotify offers copyrighted music and podcasts, including more than 60 million songs, from record labels and media companies. Since the basic features are free it is funded with advertisements. However there are paid subscriptions options available .

Sprite is a small graphic drawn independently of the rest of the screen.

SQL short for Structured Query Language and is a query language developed by IBM that uses simple English language statements to perform database queries and operations.

```
SELECT * FROM Customers WHERE CustomerName
= "Alfred";
```

In the above statement "customers" is a table and "customername" is a field in that table. The statement would return.

CustomerID	CustomerName	Address
1	Alfred	303 Jumbony Road

SRAM stands for Static Random Access Memory and is a form of RAM that retains its data without the constant refreshing that DRAM requires. SRAM is generally used for caches as it offers faster memory access times, but it is also more expensive to manufacture.

242

S-Register is the RAM in a modem that is used to store the current configuration profile.

sRGB stands for Standardised Red, Green and Blue and is the colour space standard established by the International Electrotechnical Commission which forms the basis of colour matching hardware devices such as LCD monitors, projectors, printers, scanners, digital cameras and various applications, including the World Wide Web.

SSA stands for Serial Storage Architecture and is a peripheral interface from IBM whose ring configuration allows remaining devices to function if one fails. SCSI software can be mapped over SSA allowing existing SCSI devices to be used.

SSD see Solid Sate Drive.

SSE stands for Streaming SIMD Extensions and is Intel's SSE and SSE2 technologies are effectively sets of instructions for accelerating multimedia applications. SSE is found on Intel Pentium III processors; SSE2 is an incremental supported on Intel Pentium 4 processors. Some of the benefits of SSE/SSE2 include rendering higher quality images, high quality audio, MPEG2 video, simultaneous MPEG2 encoding and decoding and reduced CPU utilisation for speech recognition. See also SIMD.

SSH stands for Stands for Secure Shell and is a protocol for secure remote login to another machine. This provides a command prompt where you can issue commands to execute programs or perform tasks on the remote machine. In Windows 10, you can connect using a program called PuTTY. You can also connect from the terminal or command prompt using the SSH command.

SSID stands for **S**ervice **S**et **ID**entifier and is the name of a WiFi network. A wireless router or access point broadcasts a SSID, allowing nearby devices to display a list of available networks.

SSL is short for Secure Sockets Layer and is a protocol used for encrypting an internet connection thereby safeguarding any data that is being sent or received. SSL uses asymmetrical cryptography which requires two cryptographic keys - one public known to everyone, one private only known by sender & receiver. You use the public key to encrypt the data, then the recipient uses the private key to decrypt it.

ST506 introduced in 1979, Seagate's ST506 was the first hard disk drive for personal computers. Supporting 5.25in full-height drives with a capacity of between 5MB and 40MB, the ST506 interface became an industry standard for the IBM PC and its successors, eventually being superseded by the IDE interface.

Start Menu is the central launch point for apps in Windows 10. Click the start button on the bottom left of the screen to open.

Start/Stop Bits are the bits at the beginning and end of a data block when using asynchronous data transmission. See also Asynchronous Communication.

STP stands for Shielded Twisted Pair and is a telephone wire that is wrapped in a metal sheath to eliminate external interference. See also UTP.

Streaming is a delivery method for transmitting data that is processed as a steady and continuous stream. Streaming allows the user to play media from the Internet without having to download the entire file first. Streaming has become popular thanks to high speed internet with many companies such as Netflix, Amazon Prime, and Apple offering on demand TV shows and films.

Subnet Mask on a TCP/IP network, is the value used to separate the IP address of a device into two parts: the network ID and the device ID. For example the IP address

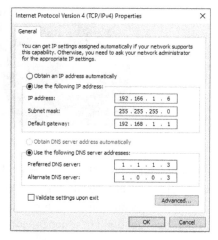

192.168.1.6

With a subnet mask of

255.255.255.0

This means that 192.168.1 is the network ID, and 6 is the device ID. This allows you to divide up large networks into smaller networks called subnets.

Sub-sampling is a bandwidth reduction technique which reduces the amount of digital data used to represent an image. Part of a compression process.

Substrate is the underlying material on which a microelectronic device or storage media is built. Silicon is the most widely used substrate for chips, fibreglass for printed circuit boards and ceramic for multichip modules. Aluminium is commonly used for hard disks, glass for optical disks and mylar for floppy disks.

Subtractive colour is created when white light is reflected off a surface that doesn't produce its own light. The surface absorbs some colours (subtracting) and reflects the remaining, thereby creating a colour. A white surface reflects all the colours, a black surface absorbs all the colours. This colour scheme commonly used in the print industry and is known as CMYK.

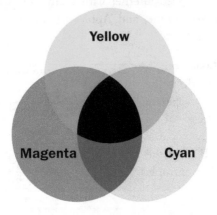

Superscalar is a CPU architecture that allows more than one instruction to be executed in one clock cycle. Processors can do this by fetching multiple instructions in one cycle, deciding which instructions are independent of other instructions, and executing them.

Surface is the top or bottom side of the platter that is coated with the magnetic material for recording data. On some drives one surface may be reserved for positioning information.

Sustained Transfer Rate is the amount of data a drive can continuously read or write per second.

SVCD or Super VCD is an evolution of the VCD format that uses MPEG-2 compression to store between 35 and 80 minutes (depending on bit rate) of SVHS quality video on a CD. Also known as Chaoji VCD.

SVGA stands for Super VGA and is a video display standard capable of handling a resolution of 800×600 256 colours, or 1024×768 16-colour support. The term was subsequently used to mean a resolution of 800×600 or greater, regardless of the number of colours available.

S-Video somewhat obsolete nowadays but was a video hardware standard used in Hi8, S-VHS video formats. It transmits luminance and colour portions separately, using multiple wires, and avoids composite video encoding which can result in loss of picture quality. Also known as Y-C Video.

Switch is a network device that operates at the data link layer (Layer 2) of the OSI reference model and whose function is to forward packets of data according to their destination address. A switch maintains a table of MAC addresses of each device connected and what port it's physically plugged into. This means the switch can forward a packet only to the port the device is connected to rather than to every port on the switch, thereby making the full bandwidth available each sender and receiver.

Switched Ethernet is an Ethernet network that is constructed using switches.

SXGA or super XGA is a screen resolution of 1280×1024 pixels, regardless of the number of colours available.

Synchronous Refers to any events that are synchronised, or co-ordinated by a regular clock pulse. Communication within a computer is usually synchronous and is governed by the microprocessor clock. Signals along the bus, for example, can occur only at specific points in the clock cycle.

Synchronous Cache is a cache that requires a clock signal to validate its control signals. This enables the cache memory to run with the CPU. Can be either Burst or Pipelined Burst.

System Bus is the primary pathway between the CPU, memory and high-speed peripherals to which expansion buses, such as ISA, EISA, PCI and VL-Bus, can connect. Also referred to as the external bus or host bus, and came to be used interchangeably with frontside bus (FSB) following the introduction of Intel's Dual Independent Bus (DIB) architecture in 1997.

T

T&L stands for Transform and Lighting and is two separate engines on the GPU that provide for a powerful, balanced PC platform and enable extremely high polygon count scenes. Transform performance determines how complex objects can be and how many can appear in a scene without sacrificing frame rate. Lighting techniques add to a scene's realism by changing the appearance of objects based on light sources.

T1 is a four-wire USA telephone company standard that carries data at 1.544Mbit/s. The US-equivalent of a European E1 line.

Tag is the subset of the CPU address bits used to compare the tag bits of the cache directory to the main memory address being accessed.

Tag RAM is a cache physically divided into two sections. The Tag RAM section stores the Tag address of the location of the data in cache. This section is smaller than the Data RAM section, which stores the actual data or instruction.

TAPI stands for Telephony Application Programming Interface and is an API that allows windows applications to program telephone-line-based devices such as modems and fax machines in a device-independent manner.

Taskbar in Windows 10, is the bar that sits along the bottom of the screen and shows which apps are currently running. You'll also see the start button on the far left. And on the far right, system status icons, the clock and action center.

TB short for Terabyte, a unit of data storage equivalent to 1 trillion bytes.

TCP/IP stands for Transmission Control Protocol/Internet Protocol and is a suite of communication protocols devices use to communicate over the internet. The TCP/IP model, like the OSI model, uses a layered approach and has four layers.

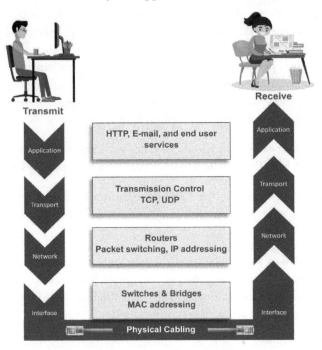

TDM stands for Time Division Multiplexing and is a data communications technique that interleaves separate data streams into one high-speed transmission by assigning each stream a different time slice in a set. The receiving end then divides the single stream back into its original constituent signals.

TDMA stands for Time Division Multiple Access and is a mobile communications technique in which a radio frequency channel is divided into time slots, each of which lasts for a fraction of a second. TDMA divides a 30KHz channel into six time slots that are allocated in pairs, resulting in three usable TDMA channels. Any given conversation can use one or more of every third time slot on an ongoing basis during a call.

Tearing is a video artefact in which portions of a video window are not updated in time for the next frame.

Teleconference is a general term for a meeting not held in person. Usually refers to a multi-party telephone call, set up by the phone company or private source, which enables more than two callers to participate in a conversation. The growing use of video allows participants at remote locations to see, hear, and participate in proceedings, or share visual data ("video conference").

Tesla Magnetic fields, or more specifically, magnetic flux densities historically have been measured with a unit called the milligauss – 1 milligauss(mg) being equal to 0.001 Gauss(g). Electrical engineers and physicists use the Tesla as a unit of international standard, one Tesla being the equivalent to 10,000 Gauss or 10,000,000 milligauss. Typically the Tesla is used in technical journals and the milligauss unit is used in information for the general public.

Tessellation is the process of dividing an object or surface into geometric primitives (triangles, quadrilaterals, or other polygons) for simplified processing and rendering.

Texel is a textured picture element. The basic unit of measurement when dealing with texture-mapped 3D objects.

Texture is a 2 dimensional bitmap pasted onto a 3D object or polygon to add realism.

Texture Filtering bilinear or trilinear filtering. Also known as sub texel positioning. If a pixel is in between texels, the program colours the pixel with an average of the texels' colours instead of assigning it the exact colour of one single texel. If this is not done, the texture gets very blocky up close as multiple pixels get the exact same texel colouring, while the texture shimmers at a distance because small position changes keep producing large texel changes.

Texture Mapping is the application of a bitmap image onto a 3D shape to create different surfaces. Texture maps can vary in size and detail, and can be pasted onto various different shapes such as cylinders, spheres, cubes and so on.

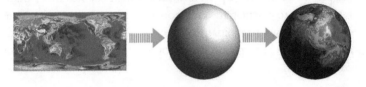

Texture Memory is used to store or buffer textures to be mapped on to 3D polygon objects.

TFT Stands for Thin Film Transistor, and is a type of LCD flat-panel display screen, in which each pixel is controlled by one to four transistors. TFT technology provides the best resolution of all the current flat-panel techniques. TFT screens are sometimes called active- matrix LCDs.

Thermal Recalibration is the periodic sensing of the temperature in hard disk drives so as to make minor adjustments to the alignment servo and data platters. In an AV drive, this process is performed only in idle periods so that there is no interruption in reading and writing long streams of digital video data.

Thermal Compound a paste often applied between a CPU and it's heatsink to ensure best possible contact and transfer of heat

Thermal Transfer is a printer technology that uses heat to transfer coloured dye onto paper.

Thermo Autochrome is a print technology used in digital camera companion printers that claimed to produce photographic quality output on a par with the more well-known dye sublimation printers.

Thin Film is a type of coating allowing very thin layers of magnetic material used on hard disks and read/write heads. Hard disks with thin film surfaces can store greater amounts of data.

Thread is the smallest executable unit of a process. A process can have multiple threads running as part of it.

TiB short for Tebibyte and is a unit of measure consisting of 1024GiB.

TIFF stands for Tagged Image File Format and is a popular file format for bitmapped graphics that stores the data in discrete blocks called tags. Each tag contains a particular attribute of the image, such as its width or height, the compression method used (if any), and a textual description of the image.

Time Code is a frame-by-frame address code time reference recorded on the spare track of a videotape or inserted in the vertical blanking interval. It is an eight-digit number encoding time in hours, minutes, seconds, and video frames (e.g.:02:04:48:26).

Time Line is a scale measured in either frames or seconds that provides an editable sequence of images, animation, and video clips to produce a final video. Here below, you can see a time line for an Adobe Premiere Video Project.

TLB short for Translation Lookaside Buffer and is a section of memory within a processor which caches part of the translation from virtual addresses to physical addresses. Also referred to as Address Translation Cache.

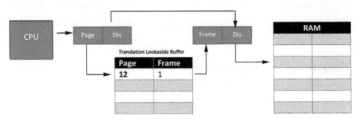

Token Ring is a local area network (LAN) technology developed by IBM (IEEE 802.5) where a special packet called a token is "passed" around the ring - only the PC with the token is allowed to send data onto the ring.

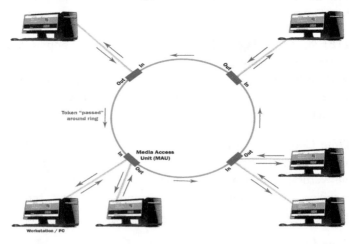

Tone Dialling is one of two methods of dialling the telephone. (The other is pulse dialling.) With tone dialling, the modem sends tones of different frequencies to represent the telephone numbers. Tone dialling is normally associated with push-button (touch-tone) phones and is also called Dual Tone Multi-Frequency (DTMF) dialling.

Toner is a fine powder used by copy machines and laser printers which consists of a dry, powdery substance that is attracted to an electrostatically charged drum, in order to create the image to be printed onto the paper.

Tracert, a command line utility used to trace the route of a packet between various hosts on a network

Topology is the pattern of interconnection between nodes in a communications network.

Toslink is a fibre optic digital audio connection used to connect a digital source component (e.g., DVD player, CD player, etc.) to a receiver or pre-amplifier. By passing the "raw" digital audio signal using laser (light) pulses, interference and degradation are minimised. The means of interconnect used for connecting MiniDisc players to stereos and certain sound cards.

TPI stands for Tracks Per Inch and is the number of tracks written within each inch of a storage medium's recording surface.

TPM or Trusted Platform Module is a chip usually mounted on the motherboard that securely stores passwords, certificates, or encryption keys that are used to authenticate a PC or laptop so that malware can't access or tamper with that data

Track is a sub-division of the recording area of storage media, such as magnetic disks, optical discs and magnetic tape.

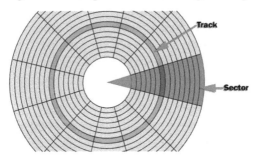

Transceiver a term used to describe a combination of transmitter and receiver. In the context of networking, a transceiver is an electronic interface or adapter between the Ethernet coaxial cable and the drop cable that attaches to network devices to provide the drive, reception, and collision detection between physical network media.

Transfer Rate is the rate at which the disk drive sends and receives data from the controller. The sustained transfer rate includes the time required for system processing, head switches, and seeks, and accurately reflects the drive's true performance. The burst mode transfer rate is a much higher figure that refers only to the movement of data directly into RAM.

Transistor is a device used to amplify a signal or open and close a circuit. In a computer, it functions as an electronic switch, or bridge. The transistor contains a semiconductor material that can change its electrical state when pulsed. Invented in 1947 at Bell Labs, transistors have become the key ingredient of all digital circuits, including computers.

Transparency is the quality of being able to see through a material. The terms transparency and translucency are often used synonymously; however, transparent would technically mean "seeing through clear glass," while translucent would mean "seeing through frosted glass."

Trichromatic is the technical name for RGB representation of colour to create all the colours in the spectrum.

Trojan is the name and concept derived from the story of the Trojan horse used to invade the city of Troy. A trojan masquerades as an ordinary program or utility that carries a hidden, more sinister function. This could be data theft, or a ransomware attack.

True Black is produced using a separate black ink rather than a mixture of cyan, magenta and yellow. See also Composite Black.

Two

True Colour is the ability to generate 16,777,216 colours (24-bit colour).

TTL stands for Time To Live and is the lifespan of data on a computer or network before being discarded.

TWAIN is an interface that enables an application to communicate with a scanner or other image capture device.

Tweening also known as in-betweening is calculating the intermediate frames between two keyframes to simulate smooth motion.

Twisted Pair is two insulated wires, usually copper, twisted together and often bound into a common sheath to form multi-pair cables. In ISDN, these cables are the basic path between a subscriber's terminal or telephone and the PBX or the central office.

Two's Complement is a binary number system that encodes positive and negative integers. The bit on the left is known as the most significant bit or MSB and is used to indicate a positive (0) or negative (1) number.

Sign	4	2	1
1	1	0	1

The remaining bits are used to store the value itself.

Decimal	Two's-complement
4	0100
3	0011
2	0010
1	0001
0	0000
-1	1111
-2	1110
-3	1101
-4	1100

To convert a binary number to two's complement, invert each bit. Add 1 to the rightmost bit (least significant bit).

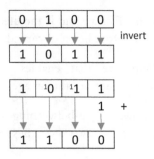

Two-Factor Authentication is an authentication method where a confirmation code is sent to the user's phone number or email address that was registered when the account was opened.

Typeface is a family of characters what have a similar design, eg, Times New Roman. See font.

U

UART stands for Universal Asynchronous Receiver Transmitter and is the chip that drives a serial port. IBM chose the National INS8250, better known simply as "the 8250", for the serial ports in its original PC. The subsequent 16550 UART provided support for speeds of 9,600 bps and greater.

UEFI stands for Unified Extensible Firmware Interface and replaces the old BIOS firmware interface on IBM-PC compatible computers.

ULSI stands for Ultra Large Scale Integration and is a chip with more than one million transistors.

Ultra DMA is a hard drive protocol which doubled the previous maximum I/O throughput to 33 MBps.

UMTS stands for Universal Mobile Telecommunications System and is a 3G standard developed under the auspices of ETSI, and intended mainly for the evolution of GSM networks.

UNC stands for Universal Naming Convention and is a standard used to locate a shared resource on a local area network. On a windows network:

```
\\server-name\shared-resource
```

On a unix/linux network

```
//server-name/shared-resource
```

Unformatted Capacity is the total number of usable bytes on a disk, including the space that will be required later to record location, boundary definitions, and timing information. See also formatted capacity.

Unicode is a universal encoding standard for representing the characters of all the languages of the world, including those with larger character sets such as Chinese, Japanese, and Korean. See UTF-8, UTF-16

Unix is a multi-user, multi-tasking operating system originally developed by Ken Thompson at AT&T Bell Labs in the late 1960s. The core of Unix is the kernel which allocates CPU time and memory to programs, handles devices and the file system. When using Unix, you interact with the operating system using a shell - a user interface where you can type in commands.

URL is short for Uniform Resource Location and describes the address of a website. For example: www.elluminetpress.com.

The URL itself can be broken down into its basic elements. Lets take a closer look at an example.

- **www** means the server hosting the service, in this case www for World Wide Web. Usually points to your public_html directory on the web server.
- **elluminetpress** is the domain name or organisation's name and is unique to that organisation.

- **.com** is the type of site. It can be .co.x for country specific companies (eg .co.uk), .org for no profit organisations, or .gov for government organisations. These are known as top level domain names and are designed to identify the types of companies represented on the web.

USB stands for Universal Serial Bus and is a standard for attaching peripherals such as printers, scanners, mice, keyboards and other equipment to a computer. The original USB1.1 standard supports a rate of 12Mbps.

USB 2 transfers data at about 480Mbps which is about 60 Megabytes per second. USB 2 is colour coded with black.

USB 3 transfers data at about 5 Gbps which is about 640 Megabytes per second. This makes them ideal for external hard drives and other high speed devices. USB 3 is colour coded with blue on the end of the plug.

USB C has a smaller connector that can be inserted either way up, and transfers data at about 10 Gbps or roughly 1.25 Gigabytes per second.

USB Drive is an external data storage device such as a portable hard disk drive, or a flash drive that can be plugged into a USB port.

USB Stick is a data storage device that uses flash memory to store data and can be plugged into a USB port.

USB-IF stands for USB Implementers Forum and is a non-profit corporation founded by the group of companies that developed the Universal Serial Bus specification to provide a support organization and forum for the advancement and adoption of USB technology. The Forum facilitates the development of high-quality compatible USB peripherals (devices), and promotes the benefits of USB and the quality of products that have passed compliance testing.

UTF-8 is a variable length encoding system that uses one to four bytes to represent a character. The '8' means it uses 8-bit blocks to represent the character. UTF-8 is backwards compatible with ASCII and widely used in internet web pages. In your HTML code you might see something like this: `<meta charset="utf-8">`. See unicode.

UTF-16 is a variable-length encoding system where each character is represented by either one or two 16-bit blocks and used in major operating systems such as Microsoft Windows, as well as in Java and .NET. See unicode.

UTP is short for Unshielded Twisted-Pair and is a four-pair wire cable used in a variety of different types of networks such as Ethernet and telephones. UTP does not require the fixed spacing between connections that is necessary with coaxial-type connections. See also STP.

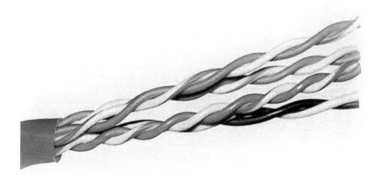

UTRAN stands for UMTS Terrestrial Radio Access Network and is the name of the WCDMA radio network in UMTS.

UV Light or Ultraviolet Light has a very short wavelengths and is just beyond the violet end of the visible spectrum. It is used to expose patterns on the layers of the microprocessor in a process much like photography.

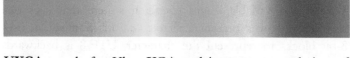

UXGA stands for Ultra XGA and is a screen resolution of 1600×1200 pixels.

V

V.34 is an ITU modem standard for data transmission at up to 33.6 Kbit/s. V.34 is the successor to several earlier ITU standards, and most V.34 modems can interoperate with older, slower modems.

V.90 is an ITU's modem standard, agreed on 4 February 1998, which brought to an end a year-long 56 Kbit/s standards battle between the rival proprietary X2 and K56Flex standards.

VAR stands for Value Added Reseller and is a company which resells hardware and software packages to developers and end users.

VBR stands for Variable Bit Rate and varies the amount of data per segment allowing a higher bit rate for more complex segments, such as more action or movement in a video, and a lower bit rate for less complex segments.

VCR stands for Video Cassette Recorder and is a videotape recording and playback machine that is available in several formats. Sony's Beta tape was the first VCR format, but is now defunct in favour of VHS which became the most commonly used format. See also VHS.

VDI stands for Video Device Interface and is a a software driver interface that improves video quality by increasing playback frame rates and enhancing motion smoothness and picture sharpness. VDI was developed by Intel and will be broadly licensed to the industry.

VDRV stands for Variable Data Rate Video and in digital systems, the ability to vary the amount of data processed per frame to match image quality and transmission bandwidth requirements. DVI symmetrical and asymmetrical systems can compress video at variable data rates.

Vector Graphics Images are defined by points on a Cartesian plane, which are connected by lines and curves to form polygons and other shapes.

Vertex is a dimensionless position in three or four-dimensional space at which two or more lines (for instance, edges) intersect.

VESA stands for Video Electronics Standards Association and is an international non-profit organisation established in 1989 to set and support industry-wide interface standards designed for the PC, workstation, and other computing environments. The VESA Local Bus (VL-Bus) standard – introduced in 1992 and widely used before the advent of PCI – was a 32-bit local bus standard compatible with both ISA and EISA cards.

VFAT stands for Virtual File Allocation Table and is the 32-bit file system that Windows 95 used to manage information stored on disks. An extension of the FAT file system, VFAT supports long filenames and 32-bit Protected Mode access while retaining compatibility with FAT volumes.

VfW stands for Video for Windows and is a standard established by Microsoft for the integration of digital video, animation and sound which uses the .AVI file format. The necessary software drivers are incorporated into the Windows operating system.

VGA also referred to as Video Graphics Adapter, it quickly replaced earlier standards such as CGA (Colour Graphics Adapter) and EGA (Enhanced Graphics Adapter) and made the 640×480 display showing 16 colours the norm. Other manufacturers have since extended the VGA standard to support more pixels and colours. See also SVGA.

VGA Feature Connector is a standard 26-pin plug for passing the VGA signal on to some other device, often a video overlay board. This feature connector cannot pass the high-resolution signal from the card and is limited to VGA.

VHS a VCR format introduced by JVC in 1976 to compete with Sony's BetaMax format. VHS subsequently become the standard for home and industry, and Beta became obsolete. S-VHS (Super VHS) is a subsequent format that improves resolution.

VidCap is Microsoft's Video For Windows program to capture video input to RAM or hard disk memory.

Video Capture is performed by an expansion card that digitises full motion video from a VCR, camera or other video source. The digital video is then stored in a compressed format on hard disk.

Video Card or graphics card is responsible for processing video, graphic and visual effects you see on your monitor. The graphics card is also known as a GPU (graphics processing unit).

Video Mapping is a feature allowing the mapping of an AVI, MPEG movie or animation on to the surface of a 3D object.

Video Memory is the RAM built onto the graphics card used for processing graphics.

Video Scaling and Interpolation When scaled upwards, video clips tend to become pixelated, resulting in block image.

Hardware scaling and interpolation routines smooth out these jagged artefacts to create a more realistic picture. Better interpolation routines work on both the X and Y axis to prevent stepping on curved and diagonal elements.

Video1 is the default video compression algorithm in Microsoft's Video for Windows. Can produce 8- or 16-bit video sequences.

VideoCD is a format that allows the viewing of MPEG-1 (also known as the ISO IEC 11172 compression standard) video on CD-ROM. Originally devised by Philips, it allows for more than an hour of compressed video, the audio also being compressed and giving hi-fi standard. The whole point of VideoCD is cross-platform compatibility. The discs should work on suitably equipped PCs, Macs, dedicated VideoCD players, and CD-i systems. Video CD is based on the White Book standard developed by Philips and other industry leaders. Also referred to as VCD.

Virtual Desktop is a feature of many modern desktop operating systems such as MacOS and Windows 10 that allows you to create multiple, separate desktops where each can display different windows and apps.

Virtual Reality is a systemy that allows the user to experience 3D interaction with the computer. Some VR systems may incorporate special visors, helmets, gloves, and special 3D graphics technology to simulate the real world environment.

Virtual Machine is a virtual or software version of a computer system. One or more virtual machines (known as guests) run on a physical machine called a host. Each guest has its own operating system, virtual processor, memory, storage, and networking.

Virtual Memory an allocated portion of a computers hard disk drive or secondary storage used as if it were main memory (RAM).

Virus is a computer virus is a piece of malicious code that replicates itself by injecting code into other programs.

Viterbi Decoder is a decoding algorithm developed in the late 1960s by Andrew Viterbi and used to decode a particular convolutional code (i.e. that adds redundancy to the data to improve the signal-to-noise ratio). Viterbi decoders output a 0 or a 1 based on an estimate of the input signal. Viterbi decoders are needed for reading HD DVD and Blu-ray discs.

VLB stands for VESA Local Bus or VL-Bus: the 32-bit local-bus standard created by the Video Electronics Standards Association (VESA) to provide a fast data connection between CPUs and local-bus devices. The VL-Bus was widely used in 486 PCs, but has since been replaced by the Intel PCI Bus.

VLSI stands for Very Large Scale Integration and is the process of placing hundreds of thousands (between 100,000 and one million) of electronic components on a single chip. Nearly all modern chips employ VLSI architectures, or ULSI (ultra large scale integration).

VM Channel stands for Vesa Media Channel, VESA's video bus which avoids the main system bus.

Voice Coil is a fast and reliable actuator that works like a loudspeaker, with the force of a magnetic coil causing a proportionate movement of the head.

Voice coils are used to move the actuator arm on a hard disk drive and are more durable than stepper counterparts since they provide higher performance.

Voice recognition is the conversion of spoken words into computer text. Speech is first digitised and then matched against a dictionary of coded waveforms. The matches are then converted into text as if the words were typed on the keyboard.

VoIP stands for Voice over IP and is the technology used to transmit voice conversations over a data network using the Internet Protocol. The data network involved might be the Internet itself, or a corporate intranet, or managed networks used by local or long distance carriers and ISPs. An example of the later would be sip trunking. The technique promises drastically reduced costs to carriers and therefore prices to end users. Also referred to as IP Telephony.

Volatile Memory is memory that loses its contents when the power is turned off. A computer's main memory, made up of dynamic RAM or static RAM chips, loses its content immediately upon loss of power. Contrast ROM, which is non-volatile memory.

Volume in the context of a hard disk drive, is a storage area usually on a partition that is formatted using a file system such as FAT or NTFS. In windows, a volume is allocated a drive letter. A single hard disk can have multiple volumes and, unlike partitions, volumes can span multiple disks. Under the ISO 9660 standard, a volume refers to a single CD-ROM or DVD disk.

Von Neumann Architecture is a computer architecture first described by John Von Neumann in 1940s based on a stored-program concept, where program instructions and data are stored in the same memory.

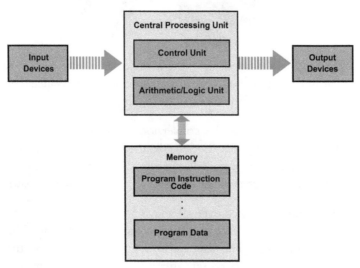

Instructions are fetched from memory one at a time and executed by the processor. Any data required by the program is fetched from memory, and any result from the execution is stored back in memory.

A processor based on Von Neumann architecture has several registers used during execution of an instruction, these are:

- Memory Address Register (MAR)

- Memory Data Register (MDR)

- Current Instruction Register (CIR)

- Program Counter (PC)

- Accumulator (ACC)

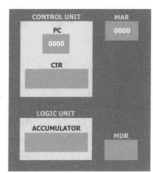

The registers and key elements of the Von Neumann architecture are used during the fetch-decode-execute cycle.

VPN stands for Virtual Private Network and is a private data network that makes use of the public telecommunication infrastructure (typically the Internet), maintaining privacy through the use of a tunnelling protocol and security procedures. It can be contrasted with a system of owned or leased lines that can only be used by one company, the idea of a VPN being to afford the same capabilities but at a much reduced cost.

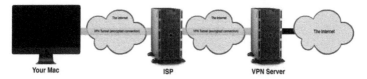

VRAM stands for Video Random Access Memory and is a dual-ported DRAM designed for graphics and video applications. One port provides data to the CRT, while the other is used for read/write transfers from the graphics controller. See WRAM.

VRM stands for Voltage Regulator Module and is used to absorb the voltage difference between a CPU which may be added in the future and the motherboard.

VRML stands for Virtual Reality Modelling Language and is a database description language applied to create 3D worlds. VRML viewers, similar to HTML Web browsers, interpret VRML data downloaded from the Web and render it on your computer. This allows the bulk of the processing to be performed locally, and drastically reduces the volume of information for transmittal from the Web.

VUMA stands for VESA Unified Memory Architecture and is a standard which establishes the electrical and logical interface between a system controller and an external VUMA device enabling them to share physical system memory.

VXD a virtual device driver.

Wafer Fab also known as a semiconductor fabrication plant is where all of a semiconductor's electronic components are interconnected onto a single die of silicon.

WAN stands for Wide Area Network and is a geographically dispersed network formed by linking several computers or local area networks (LANs) together over long distances, usually using leased long-distance lines. WANs can connect systems across town, in different cities, or in different regions of the world.

WAP stands for Wireless Application Protocol and is a protocol that enables Internet services to be delivered to small-screen mobile devices. The application via which WAP-enabled devices access Web content is referred to as a "micro-browser".

Watermark is a background image typically used to decorate and identify pages.

WAV is waveform Audio, the native digital audio format used in Windows. WAV files use the .wav file extension and allow different sound qualities to be recorded. Either 8-bit or 16-bit samples can be taken at rates of 11025Hz, 22050Hz and 44100Hz. The highest quality (16-bit samples at 44100Hz) uses 88KB of storage per second.

WaveTable Synthesis is a common method for generating sound electronically on a PC. Output is produced using a table of sound samples -actual recorded sounds – that are digitised and played back as needed. By continuously rereading samples and looping them together at different pitches, highly complex tones can be generated from a minimum of stored data without overtaxing the processor.

WCDMA stands for Wideband Code Division Multiple Access and is a 3G wideband radio technique which makes highly efficient use of radio spectrum and is capable of supporting data rates of up to 2 Mbit/s, sufficient to allow simultaneous access to several voice, video and data services at once.

Web Browser is a client application that fetches and displays Web pages and other WWW resources to the user. The most popular browsers are Microsoft's Edge, Google Chrome and Firefox.

WECA is the Wireless Ethernet Compatibility Alliance is a non-profit international association formed in 1999 to certify interoperability of wireless Local Area Network products based on IEEE 802.11 specification.

WEP stands for Wired Equivalent Privacy data encryption is defined by the 802.11 standard to prevent access to the network by "intruders" using similar wireless LAN equipment and capture of wireless LAN traffic through eavesdropping. WEP allows the administrator to define a set of respective "Keys" for each wireless network user based on a "Key String" passed through the WEP encryption algorithm. Access is denied by anyone who does not have an assigned key.

Wi-Fi is a wireless networking technology based on the IEEE 802.11 standard and is commonly used to provide wireless internet access to smartphones, tablets, laptops and computers. There are various Wi-Fi standards: 802.11a, 802.11b, 802.11g, 802.11ac, 802.11n...

Wi-Fi Protected Setup see WPS

Wi-Fi Router also known as a Wi-Fi hub, is the device that connects your smartphone, tablet, pc, chromebook or laptop to the internet. The device is usually supplied by your internet service provider and connects to your home phone line.

WiMAX stands for Worldwide Interoperability of Microwave Access and is an implementation of the IEEE 802.16 standard, WiMAX provides metropolitan area network connectivity at speeds of up to 75 Mbit/sec. WiMAX systems can be used to transmit signal as far as 30 miles.

WIMP stands for Windows Icons Mouse Pointer, or sometimes Windows Icons Menus Pointers, and is a term used to describe a user's interaction with a graphical user interface. Windows and MacOS are examples.

Winchester Disk is an early type of disk drive developed by IBM that stored 30MB and had a 30- millisecond access time. It's inventors called it a Winchester in honour of the .30-calibre rifle of the same name. Although modern disk drives are faster and hold more data, the basic technology is the same, so "Winchester" has become synonymous with "hard".

Windows 10 is a proprietary operating system developed by Microsoft for tablets, laptops, PCs, and workstations, released as part of its Windows NT family of operating systems. Windows 10 features a graphical user interface with a start menu consisting of various tiles for launching apps, a taskbar showing running apps and an action center for displaying notifications and settings, as well as a file explorer for managing files and folders..

Windows 11 is the successor to Windows 10 and introduces a new user interface along with many other features.

Windows Key is the key used in Windows to open the start menu and execute some keyboard shortcuts.

Wireframe is a 3D model constructed from lines and vertices forming a skeletal map of the 3D object. Textures, shading or motion can the be applied to build the finished 3D object. Also referred to as Polygon Mesh.

WLAN stands for Wireless LAN and is a local area network that transmits over the air typically in an unlicensed frequency band such as the 2.4GHz or 5GHz. Wireless access points (called base stations) are connected to an Ethernet switch and transmit a radio frequency over an area of over several hundred feet. See WiFi.

WMF stands for Windows Meta File and is a vector graphics format used mostly for word processing clip art.

Worm is a standalone, self replicating, malicious computer program designed to cause disruption to a network, steal data, install a back door, or even lock files in a ransomware attack.

WOSA stands for Windows Open Services Architecture and is a collection of APIs that provide standard ways for Windows applications to access databases, telephony devices, messaging services, and other services. ODBC and MAPI are two examples of APIs that fall under the WOSA umbrella.

WPA short for Wi-Fi Protected Access and is a security protocol used to secure WiFi networks using Temporal Key Integrity Protocol (TKIP).

WPA2 was introduced in 2004 as a successor to WPA, WPA2 is a security protocol used to secure WiFi networks using Advanced Encryption Standard (AES).

WPA-Enterprise also referred to as WPA-802.1X mode, is designed for enterprise networks and requires a RADIUS server for authentication.

WPA-Personal also referred to as WPA-PSK (pre-shared key) mode, is aimed at home and small office networks.

WPS stands for Wi-Fi Protected Setup and is a feature found on many home and small office internet WiFi routers. WPS was designed to make the process of connecting a device to a WiFi network much simpler. Most modern WiFi routers have a WPS button that allows you to quickly connect WiFi printers and other devices.

WRAM stands for Wndows Random Access Memory and is a form of VRAM used exclusively by Matrox Graphics. WRAM has added logic designed to accelerate common video functions such as bit-block transfers and pattern fills. It can substantially speed up certain graphical operations such as video playback and screen animation.

Write Back is data written into the cache by the CPU is not written into main memory until that data line in the cache is to be replaced. Also referred to as Copy Back.

Write Through is a technique for writing data from the CPU simultaneously into the cache and into main memory to assure coherency.

WWW is short for World Wide Web and is a collection of richly formatted graphic/hypermedia documents located on computers around the world and logically linked together by the Internet. With a graphical Web browser users can "surf" the Web by clicking highlighted words on the screen. Each click activates a hypertext link, connecting the user to another Web location identified by a URL.

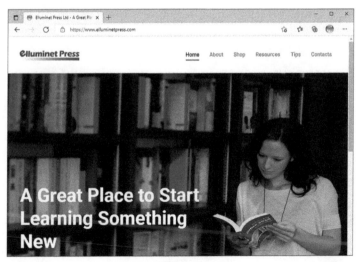

WYSIWYG stands for What You See Is What You Get and is a screen output that exactly matches the appearance when printed. WYSIWYG displays were once rare on the PC platform, because most applications ran in character mode and had little control over the format of text rendered on the screen. Today WYSIWYG applications such as Microsoft Word are common as they allow more precise control over formatting and layout without having to worry about what it will look like when printed.

X Y Z

X Windows or X11 is a windowing system developed at MIT, which runs under UNIX and all major operating systems. It uses a client-server protocol and lets users run applications on other computers on the network and view the output on their own screen.

X.10 is a communications protocol for remote control of electrical devices designed for operation over standard household electrical wiring. It transmits data using Amplitude Modulation.

X.25 is an ITU standard for packet-switching networks approved in 1976, X.25 defines layers 1, 2, and 3 in the OSI Reference Model. Such networks are widely used for point of sale (POS) terminals, credit card verifications and automatic teller machine (ATM) transactions. New packet-switched networks employ frame relay and SMDS technologies rather than X.25.

X2 is a technology developed by U.S. Robotics for achieving modem transmissions at close to 56 Kbit/s over ordinary phone lines. See also K56flex.

x64 also called x86-64, is the name for the series of 64-bit processors

x86 is a term used to describe a CPU instruction set compatible with the Intel 8086 and its successors.

xDSL stands for Digital Subscriber Line and it shares the same phone line that the telephone service uses, but because it uses a different part of the phone line's bandwidth, it does not interfere with normal phone service. This is possible because there is a significant amount of unused capacity in current phone wires. The technology will allow subscribers to hook up DSL modems to a local Internet Service Provider (ISPs) and still be able to talk on the phone – all using the same phone line. The "x" represents a variety of possible methods and information rates that can be handled through DSL.

XG is Yamaha's extension of General MIDI that provides many instrument variations and more digital effects. Many instrument parameters can be controlled in real-time.

XGA is also referred to as Extended Graphics Adapter. An IBM graphics standard introduced in 1990 that provides screen pixel resolution of 1024×768 in 256 colours or 640×480 in high (16-bit) colour. It subsequently came to be used to describe cards and monitors capable of resolutions up to 1024×768, regardless of the number of colours available.

XLR is the connector usually found on professional audio and video equipment for transmitting audio signals. Many audio mixing desks have XLR connectors to connect stage mics and instruments.

XON/XOFF is a way of controlling the flow of data between a modem and its host computer and between two modems, also called software flow control. XON stands for "Transmitter On" and XOFF stands for "Transmitter Off". If the modem receiving data needs time to process the data or do some other task, it sends an XOFF signal to the host computer (or sending modem). The host computer (or sending modem) then waits until it receives an XON signal before sending more data.

XYZ Planes are the three dimensions of space; each is designated by an axis. The x- and y-axes are the 2D co-ordinates, at right angles to each other. The z-axis adds the third dimension. Z-buffers accelerate the rendering of 3D scenes by tracking the depth position of objects and working out which are visible and which are hidden behind other objects.

YCrCb is the colour space used in the CCIR601 specification. Y is the luminance component, and the Cr and Cb components are colour difference signals. Cr and Cb are scaled versions of U and V in the YUV colour space.

YIQ is the colour space used in the NTSC colour system. The Y component is the black-and-white portion of the image. The I and Q parts are the colour components; these are effectively nothing more than a "watercolour wash" placed over the black and white, or luminance, component.

YUV is a colour encoding scheme for natural pictures in which luminance and chrominance are separate. The human eye is less sensitive to colour variations than to intensity variations. YUV allows the encoding of luminance (Y) information at full bandwidth and chrominance (UV) information at half bandwidth. YUV is used by the PAL colour system.

ZIF stands for Zero Insertion Force and is a socket allows a processor to be upgraded easily and without the need for specialist tools. It clamps down on the microprocessor pins using a small lever located to the side of the socket. Socket 5 and Socket 7 are common types of ZIF socket.

Zones Because outer tracks are longer than inner tracks they can store more data; consequently disks are divided into zones, each zone having a certain number of sectors per track.

CPSIA information can be obtained
at www.ICGtesting.com
Printed in the USA
LVHW080540130721
692490LV00011B/461